RELEASING THE POTENTIAL OF THE RISING GENERATION:
How Long-Lasting Family Enterprises Prepare Their Successors

DENNIS T. JAFFE, PH.D.

WISE COUNSEL RESEARCH
44 WINDSOR ROAD
MILTON, MA 02186

DENNIS@WISECOUNSELRESEARCH.COM
WWW.WISECOUNSELRESEARCH.COM

January, 2016

RELEASING THE POTENTIAL OF THE RISING GENERATION:
How Long-Lasting Family Enterprises Prepare Their Successors

WORKING PAPER #3
100-YEAR FAMILY ENTERPRISE RESEARCH PROJECT

DENNIS T. JAFFE, PH.D.

WISE COUNSEL RESEARCH
44 WINDSOR ROAD
MILTON, MA 02186

DENNIS@WISECOUNSELRESEARCH.COM
WWW.WISECOUNSELRESEARCH.COM

January, 2016

This working paper was sponsored by a generous donation from Merrill Lynch.

WISE COUNSEL RESEARCH
44 WINDSOR ROAD
MILTON, MA 02186

DENNIS T. JAFFE, PH.D.
DENNIS@WISECOUNSELRESEARCH.COM
WWW. WISECOUNSELRESEARCH.COM

HOW LONG-LASTING FAMILY ENTERPRISES PREPARE THEIR SUCCESSORS

Contents

WISE COUNSEL RESEARCH
44 WINDSOR ROAD
MILTON, MA 02186

DENNIS T. JAFFE, PH.D.
DENNIS@WISECOUNSELRESEARCH.COM
WWW. WISECOUNSELRESEARCH.COM

RELEASING THE POTENTIAL OF THE RISING GENERATION:

Overview

A successful multigenerational family enterprise rests on the foundation of two significant achievements—one visible and public, the other private and personal:

- In public, the family enterprise is a community icon. The founders are lauded as creative social leaders, while their children are scrutinized for how they use their privilege.

- The private, hidden success is building a great family that produces "rising" generations ready, willing and able to shoulder the emerging challenges.

A business family's public achievement cannot be sustained without the private and personal project of building a great family. A great extended family contains many households organized into several family branches that are aligned to steward a portfolio of shared assets such as a family business, family office, or family foundation. These legacy families affirm shared values and an active commitment to inspire, develop, educate and pass leadership at an opportune time to each new generation of capable and committed young people.

From interviews with members of more than 70 family enterprises from 20 countries that have moved into the third generation and beyond, this paper enters their private worlds to show how they go about building a great family with sustained wealth and active, responsible, engaged and effective successors. Our goal is to describe—using their own words—what these special families actually do to develop new generations of engaged leaders. We believe this description will help families who have achieved public, business success also succeed at the second, less visible, task: to develop and empower their rising generation.

GENERATIVE FAMILIES: THE 100 – YEAR FAMILY ENTERPRISE RESEARCH PROJECT

This is the third paper in on-going research that opens the curtain on the private worlds of the most long-lasting and successful global family enterprises.[1] To celebrate their resiliency and hardiness we call them *generative* or *legacy families*. They are *generative* because rather than deplete or consume, they add to and amplify the various forms of family wealth. **A generative family uses its resources not just to sustain what they have, but to create something new, extending their legacy—their values and practices—in new directions that add not just to the family financial wealth, but also its human, social, relationship and spiritual "capitals".** We want to learn as much as we can about how this impactful and wonderful achievement occurs, so that more families can duplicate their success. While most of these families began with a legacy business, we view them here as evolving **families,** not just businesses, sharing a changing portfolio of assets and business ventures.

---

1 The first working paper, **Three Pathways to Evolutionary Survival: Best Practices of Successful, Global, Multi-Generational Family Enterprises** (2012), presented survey data from 200 families. The second paper, **Good Fortune: Building a Hundred Year Family Enterprise** (2013) was an overview of the evolution of these families over generations. Both papers are available from Wise Counsel Research (wisecounselresearch.org).

WISE COUNSEL RESEARCH
44 WINDSOR ROAD
MILTON, MA 02186

DENNIS T. JAFFE, PH.D.
DENNIS@WISECOUNSELRESEARCH.COM
WWW. WISECOUNSELRESEARCH.COM

HOW LONG-LASTING FAMILY ENTERPRISES PREPARE THEIR SUCCESSORS

A "generative family" in our study met three criteria:

1. **Business/Financial Success.** They created a successful business, or set of enterprises, with current annual revenues of more than US$200M (with the average family's net worth being much greater). Half the families had sold their legacy business, and transitioned to become a family office, often including a family foundation.

2. **Adaptability Over Generations.** They successfully navigated at least two generational transitions, with control being passed to the third generation or later.

3. **Shared Family Identity.** They retained shared connection and identity, with practices and processes that sustained their values as an extended family.

Generative families are both very rare and very special. Few business families survive as a shared enterprise to a second or third generation. These families uphold their coherence, partnership and family connection against the tides of dispersion and separation. We estimate that fewer than 1% of family enterprises become generative in these ways. But their impact is great in that these families manage a large percentage of global wealth and perform great services to their communities. In this study we turn to these families as *teachers*, helping other successful families learn what they can do to sustain their success and connection across generations.

In each subject family our research team interviewed one member of the older and younger generations. To illustrate what they actually do as a successful extended family this paper presents their direct words. Their stories illustrate how they have thrived not just as a loving and connected family, but what they did to produce new generations of committed, active innovators, adding capability, complexity, and new directions to the expanding extended family.

WHO IS THIS PAPER FOR?

While these generative families are all moving past their third generation, their stories are relevant to the much greater number of families who are now moving into the second generation. The conditions for our subject families' success were set early on, when they made the first decision to develop their rising generation. Often it was choices made by the second generation that set the family on a generative path. While the activities described in Part Three of the paper may seem less relevant to a second generation family, the process of holding annual family meetings, educating and preparing the young members of their third generation for leadership can help position first or second generation business families for transition to the third generation.

WISE COUNSEL RESEARCH
44 WINDSOR ROAD
MILTON, MA 02186

DENNIS T. JAFFE, PH.D.
DENNIS@WISECOUNSELRESEARCH.COM
WWW. WISECOUNSELRESEARCH.COM

RELEASING THE POTENTIAL OF THE RISING GENERATION:

OUTLINE
The working paper has four parts:

Part One: The Opportunity and Challenge of Generative Families.
Looking from the perspective of the rising generation that follows earlier successful generations, this section outlines the enormous task facing each new generation to sustain and add to all aspects of the family "capitals." The key challenges of creating a life path, sustaining capital, and developing leadership in the family is a full plate for this generation.

Part Two: Developing Character in the Wealthy Household.
We explore the influence of the household (of parents, brothers and sisters, grandparents, and cousins) on the rising generation. How do these privileged families avoid the pitfalls of entitlement and raise children who, despite their wealth, are able to offer new leadership to take the family forward? We look at the informal ways that the rising generation develop a positive identity, take on shared values, and seek employment and livelihood.

Part Three: The Family Community as a Learning System.
How do these families offer education and developmental opportunities for their children, so that they are ready to enter and perform well as stewards of the family assets? We look at the role of service and values in sustaining the commitment of each new generation. This section presents the extensive and creative ways that legacy families develop programs, activities and support for rising generation growth and development.

Part Four: Calls to Service of the Rising Generation.
The "calls" to serve the Family, Business and Community inspire the new generation to commit to the family enterprise, in addition to developing their own lives. When nurtured and invited, the rising generation is a powerful resource to further develop the family legacy to add to the family, business and social capital.

WISE COUNSEL RESEARCH
44 WINDSOR ROAD
MILTON, MA 02186

DENNIS T. JAFFE, PH.D.
DENNIS@WISECOUNSELRESEARCH.COM
WWW. WISECOUNSELRESEARCH.COM

HOW LONG-LASTING FAMILY ENTERPRISES PREPARE THEIR SUCCESSORS

A Note on Terminology

The family enterprise is an unusual type of family. To make our paper clearer, here are definitions of common terms we use:

What is a Family Enterprise?

A family who shares ownership and control over various assets that can include a legacy business, new businesses, a family office, vacation and investment property, and a family foundation. By the third generation, the enterprise has many elements that may or may not include the original "legacy business," the source of family wealth.

What is a Generative, or Legacy, Family?

The whole extended family that has created a thriving family enterprise, with the intention of having family involvement across generations, with continuity of values and family commitment. It consists of multiple, individual "households" which also identify as part of one of several family branches, stemming from their connection to siblings of the second generation. Another term for a generative family is "business family" indicating that the family is engaged in not just one but often multiple, and changing, ventures.

How do we Number and Identify Generations?

By convention, the financial wealth creators form the founding generation or G1. Each successive generation has a new number: G2, G3, G4, etc. indicating generations following the creation of shared family financial wealth.

What do we call the "Next" Generation?

As each generation grows up, we will call them, somewhat interchangeably, the rising[2], emerging, next or successive generation. We call their growing children "heirs" or "successors," depending on whether we are referring to their role as inheritors or their role as emerging family and business leaders.

---

2 This term by Hughes, James, Massenzio, Susan, and Whitaker, Keith. (2014). **The Voice of the Rising Generation**. Wiley.

WISE COUNSEL RESEARCH
44 WINDSOR ROAD
MILTON, MA 02186

DENNIS T. JAFFE, PH.D.
DENNIS@WISECOUNSELRESEARCH.COM
WWW. WISECOUNSELRESEARCH.COM

RELEASING THE POTENTIAL OF THE RISING GENERATION:

Part I: The Opportunity and Challenge of Generative Families

I must study Politicks and War that my sons may have liberty to study Mathematicks and Philosophy. My sons ought to study mathematicks and philosophy, geography, natural history, naval architecture, navigation, commerce, and agriculture, in order to give their children a right to study painting, poetry, musick, architecture, statuary, tapestry, and porcelaine.
– John Adams, Letter to Abigail Adams, May 12, 1780.

You do not inherit a family business; you borrow it from your grandchildren.
– Hermes family 5th generation heir.

Every family faces the daunting challenge of raising children to become productive members of society. But following the adage "to whom much is given, much is expected," an extraordinarily wealthy family with many shared assets faces an additional challenge. They need to educate and prepare the next generation to take care of their assets as well as the freedom and opportunities they have been given to make a vital contribution. No family wants to feel that they created great wealth so that their children could be lazy, unproductive and spend it as fast as possible.

Meeting this challenge involves more than good intentions and a trust with restrictive spending rules. Our group of more than 70 generative families adopted family development practices that we believe are even more difficult, time- and energy-intensive, and demanding than creating a successful business. That may be why there are so few of them.

Families without a legacy business or substantial shared assets handle the tasks of raising productive offspring privately, within the nuclear family, preparing them to go their own way in life. The same is true for generative families, with an additional wrinkle: Given their shared resources, generative families need responsible and competent family members to steward these resources in future generations. They must teach additional skills and instill sensitivity in their successors as stewards of the family wealth, or risk losing it through inattention or incompetence.

The generative family faces a dual purpose for developing the next generation:

● Effectively use family resources to develop the potential and capability of each individual.

● Develop and install a cadre of successors to carry on the family legacy of profitable and productive enterprises.

Many of our families feel that the primary responsibility for these tasks belongs in each individual household. As one leader observed, "Our different families have different perspectives on how much information people should be provided with and in terms of the attitudes towards money and spending and what kids should have or not have. And so those kinds of things are left much more to the individual families or branches." The extended family then builds on the foundation of values and character with shared family activities agreed to by everyone, designed to add specific skills and commitment to the family enterprises.

WISE COUNSEL RESEARCH
44 WINDSOR ROAD
MILTON, MA 02186

DENNIS T. JAFFE, PH.D.
DENNIS@WISECOUNSELRESEARCH.COM
WWW. WISECOUNSELRESEARCH.COM

HOW LONG-LASTING FAMILY ENTERPRISES PREPARE THEIR SUCCESSORS

BUILDING A GREAT FAMILY

A major finding of our **100-Year Family Enterprise Research Project** is that a generative family is created through two major achievements. First, members of such a family develop a great business and family financial wealth. The second achievement is committing resources, time and energy to build a great family. This second is the topic of this paper. We will see how creating a great family demands active investment to develop a new level of activity, skill and commitment. One 3rd generation family leader reflects:

You have to take the time to develop each member to their potential. People don't understand how important education is, and underestimate the time, the care and the devotion that it takes to build a strong family. But for me that's where everything happens. So that's where we spent most of our time. If you look at our family business, it would be a combination of individuation combined with collectivism.

An Asian family leader explains the many facets of this "project":

The important matters are entry of a generation, what we expect heirs to do, values we wish for the parents to instill in their kids, the role of the family in matters, and the access to the foundation programs. If they want to get involved, we have summer jobs where the kids get a birds-eye view, whether they're in high school or grade school. We have community projects; we send some of our kids to do hospital work or Habitat for Humanity. We give them a flavor of the business stuff that we think are important.

The wealth created by the generative family is more than just financial. While financial capital is important, true family "wealth" arises from other sources that also add value to the family. A great family is engaged in expanding non-financial capital, such as:

- **Human Capital:** Added value of the knowledge, skill and dedication of each family member. (Sometimes identified as Intellectual Capital.)

- **Relationship Capital:** Added value arising from the connection, care, organization and mutual support of family members.

- **Social Capital:** Added value of the family's many contributions to the community around them, including the environment.

- **Spiritual Capital:** Added value that comes from the reservoir of commitment to a deeper purpose and legacy of values.

Generative families were clear that their goal for the next generation was to develop all types of family capital.

Expanding family capital demands more than individual households teaching and preparing their children. The many households that comprise the multi-generational family enterprise also work together as an extended family group — a "tribe." They create joint educational, service and personal development activities that enable members of the rising generation to develop personal capabilities and shared teamwork, in order to work together to steward and add to the family resources. The next generation does not just inherit; it also contributes and creates.

WISE COUNSEL RESEARCH
44 WINDSOR ROAD
MILTON, MA 02186

DENNIS T. JAFFE, PH.D.
DENNIS@WISECOUNSELRESEARCH.COM
WWW. WISECOUNSELRESEARCH.COM

RELEASING THE POTENTIAL OF THE RISING GENERATION:

In these days of social mobility, the existence of these connected multi-generational tribes of closely connected related families, is highly unusual. In fact, few families are actively engaged with each other in this way, except for infrequent visits and family reunions. When a first generation wealth creator starts a business, he or she has no idea that this sort of connected family might be formed in the future. But the essence of the special nature of generative families lies in the development of these tribal entities, by creating intricate family organizations and working together on a variety of shared cross-generational family and business related activities.

My colleague James Grubman and I[3] have previously described the journey of a family that is new to wealth. Wealth creators usually come from modest circumstances, and are new **immigrants** to the experience and use of wealth. They are self-made and remember what they had to do to achieve their wealth—hard work, individual initiative, personal drive, and high control. When they look ahead to what they want their children to learn, they tend to emphasize these skills of independent action which served them well. Their intention is fine but their knowledge of the needs of the next generation is incomplete.

Their children, and grandchildren, we notice, are usually born into an environment of family affluence. They are **natives** to family wealth; it is always part of their lives and they grow up in a world of wealth that conditions their everyday reality. But they are also aware that they did not create it. They usually lack awareness of where it came from, and have anxiety about what they would do if it were not there. They hear from their parents that they should be prepared to go their own way, but because they have grown up in an affluent household, this awareness may be more theoretical than realistic. Section Two presents the nature of their learning journey experience.

In addition to learning how to find their way in work, career and personal relationships, young family members of generative families need to learn about additional areas related to their family assets and wealth. These are the subject of this paper. Because their family is linked by trusts and shared financial entities, they must learn skills to oversee and manage these assets, and how to work together in harmony, with siblings, cousins and spouses. They need collaborative and team-oriented skills to oversee, steward and add to the family capital.

WHAT IS NEEDED IN THE RISING GENERATION?
Substantial family wealth is a great challenge as well as opportunity to the next generation. While they pursue their own path in life, the many possible forms of shared family "capital" present family members with some inviting opportunities. In addition to the legacy businesses and investments, there is the possibility of founding new ones. Heirs can look beyond personal benefit in their gift from prior generations. There are also service opportunities arising from family or philanthropy. But to be useful, each successor has to develop professional skills and a personal commitment.

---

3 Jaffe, D. and Grubman, J. (Fall, 2007). *Acquirers and Inheritors Dilemma.: Finding Life Purpose and Building Personal Identity in the Presence of Wealth, Journal of Wealth Management*. This model was amplified and described in greater detail in Grubman's book **Strangers in Paradise** (2013), Family Wealth Consulting.

WISE COUNSEL RESEARCH
44 WINDSOR ROAD
MILTON, MA 02186

DENNIS T. JAFFE, PH.D.
DENNIS@WISECOUNSELRESEARCH.COM
WWW. WISECOUNSELRESEARCH.COM

HOW LONG-LASTING FAMILY ENTERPRISES PREPARE THEIR SUCCESSORS

What skills and capabilities are needed in the rising generation of a legacy family? Since the family enterprise looms large in the family psyche, their active focus on preparing for leadership takes three major forms.

- **Business:** In the second and third generation, family successors emerge who can work in the business (whether as an executive or on the board of directors). By the third generation, the family has often either sold the legacy business or transitioned to a role where they oversee the business as owners with non-family leaders to guide the company. With a family office or extensive investments, the role of board member, trustee or steward of assets demands different kinds of family leadership.

- **Family.** By the third generation, with many households comprising the extended family, successive generations must take active roles sustaining family connection and promoting cooperative relations and shared family activities to align, inspire and educate the extended family. If this does not take place, the shared commitment of the family tends to dissipate.

- **Community.** Family resources lead to many opportunities to serve the wider community, by partly supporting service careers and by initiating philanthropic and social entrepreneurship ventures.

Each of these roles is complex and demanding, but the family has a limited talent pool. They must take steps to reap the most from each person, by educating, guiding, inspiring and inviting the most talented of the next generation into leadership.

Members of G3 or G4 growing up in separate households widely dispersed geographically may not know each other personally or feel very connected to the family legacy or business unless they are actively engaged. In order to function as a unit, the generative family must renew its shared identity as a family enterprise, uniting many households.

Multi-generational legacy families do not necessarily include **all** blood family descendants. Households and family branches may drop out of the shared entity, while young people and new spouses enter. Each individual member, and the family as a whole, must develop a positive identity and reason for working as partners in the future. Family efforts are directed at using their resources to motivate and focus growing numbers of family members. "Generativity" means that the next generation does not rest on past success but commits to do more. For example, the next generation may take the business in new directions, perhaps starting new ventures that express the family's values in areas like social investment and entrepreneurship.

At some time, every member of the new generation must make a choice—to commit to the future of the whole family, or to exit, and go his or her own way. Generative families provide the opportunity to say "no" to the extended family. In every generation, some may take this opportunity to go their own way.

WISE COUNSEL RESEARCH
44 WINDSOR ROAD
MILTON, MA 02186

DENNIS T. JAFFE, PH.D.
DENNIS@WISECOUNSELRESEARCH.COM
WWW. WISECOUNSELRESEARCH.COM

RELEASING THE POTENTIAL OF THE RISING GENERATION:

2

Desired Capabilities in the Rising Generation

Legacy families have already created a thriving business and extensive wealth. Their expectations for their children are similarly broad. They want their children to be prepared to pursue their own calling or contribute to the family enterprise and to society. From their accounts, we generated a set of desired capabilities ("C's") that their education and development programs aim for:

- **Character**—ethical sensitivity

- **Competence/Capability**—financial and governance/ownership skills

- **Commitment/Caring** -–stewardship; to be a productive part of family, a good partner

- **Connections/Community**—building trust, personal commitment to each other

- **Collaboration/Compromise**—ability to work together with give and take

- **Communication/Transparency**—sharing information, understanding what there is

- **Change-ability/Resilience**—ability to adapt and change

- **Curiosity/Creativity**—ability to seek out and discover novel possibilities

Great families see their rising generation as future leaders, and train and develop them with both personal and professional skills. It is no easy task to develop these leadership capabilities in several next generation family leaders. A person with all these qualities might sound like a super-hero! This looks like the wish list for a corporate leadership development program, which it is. All the efforts we describe, from individual family learning to shared educational and development programs, are aimed at this level of development of leaders whose role is that of a family "steward." These outsized expectations for the next generation can be inspiring but also overwhelming. The key is to create programs that offer the right amount of challenge.

FAMILY AND WEALTH: A TANGLED WEB

"It's all about the money" a family leader observes. While this view is held by many family elders, generative families for the most part view this notion as short-sighted. Although money looms large in the life choices of a next generation family member, continuity depends on developing all forms of family capital. Money alone is not a strong enough glue to compel family members to dedicate themselves to each other.

Inheriting wealth does not mean a person has the ability to use it wisely. It must be learned.

While there are many reasons why families remain connected over generations, the promise and expectation of sharing in the family wealth is at the top of the list of motivators. Financial rewards are not just for immediate enjoyment, but also to be sustained for future generations and used for values-based endeavors. Family members must develop a balance between current and future needs, and between consumption and service.

WISE COUNSEL RESEARCH
44 WINDSOR ROAD
MILTON, MA 02186

DENNIS T. JAFFE, PH.D.
DENNIS@WISECOUNSELRESEARCH.COM
WWW. WISECOUNSELRESEARCH.COM

HOW LONG-LASTING FAMILY ENTERPRISES PREPARE THEIR SUCCESSORS

By remaining united across generations and reinvesting profits, even with many family members, the family enterprise can become quite large and profitable. At some point, often at the initiative of the emerging generation, the family begins to ask what all this family wealth is to be used for? This young successor in a hundred-year old South Asian family with 450 family members observes:

The first 80 years were basically surviving and building up wealth; we reached the point where we're doing very well—more cash flow, higher dividends. With more wealth, there could be a change in behavior with the way the younger generation deals with it, so we have to be very conscious about how this wealth is deployed and how we manage to keep our values in the midst of all of this seeming success.

One of the most important practices for a family entering the third generation is that they develop and affirm a set of values and purposes for their various family enterprises and their wealth. They have to answer the question, "What is our financial wealth for?' in a way that engages the members of the rising generation. The presence of shared values and mission is necessary so that the family, with new members entering regularly by birth and marriage, agrees about what it is doing together.

With so many family members the expectation of living a life of ease is not realistic. Aside from a very few (but highly visible) members of the global leisure class, 4th or 5th generation family heirs can look forward to a nice "lifestyle supplement" to their income, enabling them for example, to work for a lower salary in a rewarding career, but not enough to not work at all:

(Family wealth) enabled me to live comfortably and put my kids through college. My kids definitely see it in the same way. My son owns his own business. I have given him a lot of support, but he knows it comes from our family business. The family definitely sees that. And that is our success; not only that but the family stories are continuing.

Young children growing up in a wealthy environment cannot be expected to understand these limits; the family has to help them overcome unrealistic under- or over-estimates of family financial wealth.

Families have different ways of distributing wealth. Each approach deeply influences the mindset, motivation and development of the rising generation. Traditional cultures, spanning regions such as southern Europe, the Middle East, and South America, offer an allowance or regular distribution to each family member, usually allocated by age. Only a handful of our legacy families operated this way, and they all reported finding this approach counter-productive. *When income is not connected with ownership or family engagement, its presence gives the message that there is nothing the rising generation need to do to qualify for it. It makes family organization more difficult.* The majority of our families pass inheritance to individual households; each household or family branch allocates inheritance. One legacy family can therefore have several approaches to inheritance.

WISE COUNSEL RESEARCH
44 WINDSOR ROAD
MILTON, MA 02186

DENNIS T. JAFFE, PH.D.
DENNIS@WISECOUNSELRESEARCH.COM
WWW. WISECOUNSELRESEARCH.COM

RELEASING THE POTENTIAL OF THE RISING GENERATION:

G1 wealth creators usually create a complex set of financial structures—trusts, holding companies, and foundation—which form the reality for each successive generation. As one sociological researcher observes:

> In generational aging and transition, a family must create a transcendent, controlling version of itself in the organization of its property to achieve a coherence of organization that can preserve the mystique of its name and ensure its continuing exercise of patrician functions in its social environment. This coherence does not come as much from commitments made by its members to their common lineage, as from the application of law and the work of fiduciaries whose primary responsibility is to protect the founder's legacy from divisive family quarrels.[4]

Between the heir and the family wealth, then, lie trusts and financial entities, as well as family advisors, that heirs must understand, accept, navigate and eventually, oversee. Young people, learning about this legal structure, can feel devalued or distrusted if for example, they are offered a beneficiary role with limited power or influence. The successful family must provide the training to make this relationship harmonious and satisfying, and maybe find ways to allow more flexibility. Each young family member must understand these options and learn how to relate to them in a mutually beneficial manner, that may not be immediately clear. By understanding, negotiating and being engaged, they may discover areas of flexibility not initially apparent. To avoid acrimony and conflict, the family must develop caring relationships and commitment to work together so that the family wealth serves the family goals.[5]

With the growing family infrastructure of shared activities and practices, a young person growing up in a wealthy household can't help but wonder about the family wealth. They wonder about…

- What they can expect in their lives,

- The rules for using and benefiting from the family resources,

- What the family enterprise contains, and how it works,

- Roles they might look forward to in the business and family, and

- What they have to do to attain them.

The family can constructively engage this curiosity and offer answers so that the young heir can move forward with his or her life and make thoughtful and relevant decisions.

Family wealth, we suggested earlier, also includes the human, relationship, social and spiritual capital. This can endure longer than the original financial wealth; in fact, developing other forms of capital can offer meaning and purpose to the family, as well as lead to additional financial wealth.

---

4 Marcus, George. (1992). **Lives in Trust.** Westview Press, p. 55

5 The new book by Hartley Goldstone, James Hughes, and Keith Whitaker, **Family Trusts** (2015; Wiley), explains the opportunity to expand this relationship.

WISE COUNSEL RESEARCH
44 WINDSOR ROAD
MILTON, MA 02186

DENNIS T. JAFFE, PH.D.
DENNIS@WISECOUNSELRESEARCH.COM
WWW. WISECOUNSELRESEARCH.COM

HOW LONG-LASTING FAMILY ENTERPRISES PREPARE THEIR SUCCESSORS

THE FAMILY ENTERPRISE OPPORTUNITY

Legacy families want to see their children develop positive personal identity, expressed values and meaningful, productive lives. The rising generation must also prepare for roles in service to the family. The larger challenge for the family is to develop the capability and desire—the "will" and "skill"—to take on various family and family enterprise leadership roles. All these challenges fall to the emerging young family members.

A single family successor, within the rising generation, is expected in many parts of the world. But this expectation is changing as more families take a broader view of their family leadership needs. Generative families look at the capability of the shared generation as a collective resource; several family members emerge in different leadership roles, for example, in the business, the family and philanthropy. The many members of the next generation want to understand how to develop leadership capability and how they will be recognized.

Globally, the traditional expectation of ascension by the eldest son is being replaced with an expectation that each member of the new generation would make his or her own choice about their candidacy. Leaders are selected from this self-defining group. One elder remarked:

> I don't want my kids to feel an obligation to work here. They certainly need to feel the responsibility that ownership brings, and that responsibility is there whether they cash out or own everything. There's a responsibility that comes with life that they need to learn. The degree to which they are involved, I do not want to try to dictate nor even premeditate. All I want is the flexibility for them to pursue what turns them on and to try to live the best life they can.

The resounding view is that no young family member should feel coerced into partnership. As one family put it, there should be a "free choice" to choose one's role in relation to family assets, or even to leave the partnership. This is made more complicated by the formation of trusts that can tie them together for a generation or two. But by the third or fourth generation—in all of our generative families—there is a mechanism to "free" dissident family members. This **exit policy** is a resolution for potential conflict that can otherwise tie up a family and make it difficult for them to function as a coherent business. Knowing they can always leave, sometimes family members can then agree to remain and see what they can achieve together.

Most families expect their adult children to go off and "seek their fortune." In a legacy family the fortune is already there, posing a challenge and an opportunity. Our research made us aware that the rising generation of a legacy family must decide how actively and directly they want to be engaged with the family and its enterprises. Family education offers a grounding for making informed choices.

This is not a single choice, but a reality that lies before them as they become responsible and productive adults. We see them making life choices in relation to the family, as they answer the following questions for themselves:

- How do I responsibly draw on the family wealth?

- How will I be involved and engaged with the family and its enterprises?

WISE COUNSEL RESEARCH
44 WINDSOR ROAD
MILTON, MA 02186

DENNIS T. JAFFE, PH.D.
DENNIS@WISECOUNSELRESEARCH.COM
WWW. WISECOUNSELRESEARCH.COM

RELEASING THE POTENTIAL OF THE RISING GENERATION:

- Will I initiate or get involved in family supported philanthropic and community ventures?

- Will I take on a leadership role in some aspect of the family enterprise?

To consider "joining" the family enterprise, or how much to be involved in governance, each young family member has to first spend some time outside the family. Going off on their own, working outside the family, is one of the most common early developmental steps mentioned by our families. Absent a crisis, most families discourage family members from entering the business too soon:

> *I think the ones that are successful have done it by moving outside as they transition into adulthood, through college and all that, in particular when it comes to business. To be outside the family, live on your own, do your own thing, find your own friends, move out of town. One of the most important things that all of my nieces and nephews have done and I hope what my daughter does is that she gets a paycheck for a few years from somebody else to prepare her for what the real world is like.*

Only a few family members can be employed by various family enterprises, and the family wants to make sure that they select the most capable, and those with the best "fit," who are prepared to serve. By then, there is room in the business for only a few family members. Most third- and later-generation successors draw upon the advantages of education and social contacts to develop independent careers. These careers are often aided by supplementary income from the family, which allow them to work below market rates on something they care about:

> *One family member formed his own music label and now runs that. Another started his own non-profit and another was in the early stages of forming a larger non-profit. So many people have been able to take that philanthropic ball and run with it, because they have the flexibility for the plans and perspective to do what they wanted to do and pursue that passion.*

Lessons learned at home and on their personal journey help develop personal capability and life direction. But the legacy family offers uncountable opportunities. With so many possibilities, they need guidance to discover and channel them:

> *Our biggest "idea bin" is trying to find an opportunity for future generations. It's more of an intellectual than a physical opportunity. We have a dozen fifth generation family members between 16 and 26 and through my parents' leadership, their parents (of which I'm in that generation and I have an 11-year-old) feel this tremendous need to look at developing opportunities for them. We're not trying to pick their job or buy a business they like. We're trying to bring them into a mix that says you have an important tool in life that allows you to make a better life for yourself. The family business provides some resources the fourth generation put it in a package that younger kids in G5 see as a meaningful opportunity.*

WISE COUNSEL RESEARCH
44 WINDSOR ROAD
MILTON, MA 02186

DENNIS T. JAFFE, PH.D.
DENNIS@WISECOUNSELRESEARCH.COM
WWW. WISECOUNSELRESEARCH.COM

HOW LONG-LASTING FAMILY ENTERPRISES PREPARE THEIR SUCCESSORS

In return for being offered special opportunities, each young person is asked implicitly to develop credibility and demonstrate capability within the family. Family membership adds pressure to making life and career choices; it never makes these choices easier. Here is one account from a G5 entering business leadership along with his generational peers:

> When I started working I was thrown in the deep end. (To enter our family business) you have to have some store of experience, build a business, etc. Your responsibility grows as you show your capability. I worked outside for a few years at a private equity fund. Then I came back into the family business. When I came back, I could see that few of our larger, global businesses had someone involved from the younger generation. So, I told my uncle who's driving those businesses 'I'd like to get involved.' I came on board as the next generation guy.

> I've been in those businesses now for 15 years and my uncle is still there; he's 70-something now. I've proven myself, built my credibility. At the last executive committee meeting I told them, 'Listen, the last few meetings he'd been absent, and I'd effectively chaired them.' So, for one specific businesses 'I've already done this and maybe it's time that you let me do this and you can add or comment afterwards if I've missed anything.' He actually said 'Okay' and the next meeting he stepped back and said 'You drive it.' It's not easy, these guys don't like to let go. You have to push them a little. If they're comfortable, they'll step back. It's not easy; they still meddle around once in a while. But the CEO of that business passed away. The new CEO got the message that I'm the guy who's driving it so he calls me now. The transition happened over 15 years. It didn't happen overnight.

The next section of our paper looks at personal development as it begins with learning by example inside the household, followed by a personal journey of self-discovery out in the world. With this foundation, a young family member in a legacy family is ready to take advantage of the opportunities provided by the extended family, and make a choice whether to answer the "call" to become active in the family enterprise, and take on a leadership or active role.

APPLYING WHAT YOU LEARNED: QUESTIONS FOR FAMILY REFLECTION

These questions can be posed to family members, to begin a conversation related to the key ideas presented in Part One:

For the Elder Generation:	For the Rising Generation:
• What do you want from the rising generation?	• What do you want from your parents and elders?
• What have you been doing to help the rising generation achieve what you expect from them? How can you help them move in that direction?	• What do you think they expect from you?
• What process are you going to use to select the next generation of family leadership?	• What are you doing to prepare for your career and life goals?

WISE COUNSEL RESEARCH
44 WINDSOR ROAD
MILTON, MA 02186

DENNIS T. JAFFE, PH.D.
DENNIS@WISECOUNSELRESEARCH.COM
WWW. WISECOUNSELRESEARCH.COM

RELEASING THE POTENTIAL OF THE RISING GENERATION:

PART II: DEVELOPING CHARACTER IN THE WEALTHY HOUSEHOLD

The primary responsibility of parents is to raise productive adults. If the family is also an economic unit, the family usually prepares their children to fulfill their responsibilities in the family enterprises. This task is made more difficult when the family has substantial wealth. Wealth can be seductive; it deeply affects the reality of how children grow up and learn that the wealth is not just something to make them special and comfortable. The family has to teach values about their responsibility to be a steward of the wealth, insuring that it will be used wisely.

An added challenge is that wealthy children grow up with a sense of specialness that sometimes translates into feeling that wealth makes them better than other people. This is called **entitlement**; its opposite, a sense of service and responsibility to sustain the wealth and add to it, we call **stewardship**. The goal of the privileged household is to help its children move from entitlement to stewardship. This section explores two facets of this endeavor: first the active role of parents before their children begin university; then the journey of the young adult to develop a personal identity. The first one is the prime time for active family engagement, teaching and learning, followed by a period of gradually letting go as young adults find their way through higher education and into their first work experiences.

PARENTING IN THE HOUSEHOLD

Parents set examples about values and teach responsibility even when they are not conscious they are doing so. "Messages" are passed in family conversations about what is and is not important about wealth and in life. For example, one young women proudly showed her father her first paycheck, from working in a service project. Her father's response was, "Why are you working. You don't have to work." The effect of this message was that she always felt vaguely guilty about working, because she was taking money away from people who needed it.

Young people develop values from their parents' indirect messages and examples. They may learn that a person's worth is measured by how much money they have, or that people who have money do or do not do certain things. These messages can be conscious or unconscious.

Money has many meanings for a young person. Children are especially curious about where money comes from, as it is very abstract and almost magical. They have to learn that some people do not have nice houses and schools. Their experience may be that when you want money, just stop at an ATM and get some. Parents may use money as a reward, or give children gifts when they go off to travel, leaving their children to learn that money can be a barely adequate substitute for love and engagement.

WISE COUNSEL RESEARCH
44 WINDSOR ROAD
MILTON, MA 02186

DENNIS T. JAFFE, PH.D.
DENNIS@WISECOUNSELRESEARCH.COM
WWW. WISECOUNSELRESEARCH.COM

HOW LONG-LASTING FAMILY ENTERPRISES PREPARE THEIR SUCCESSORS

Values, our families report, arise from engagement and example within the family, rather than policies and rules. Here is an account by a South American family of how one parent influenced his kids:

I raised my children to be leaders, and live by the family values. We started working with the children when they were very young. We went with them to sports activities and every single day of my life I talked to every single child. Every night we'd have a little chat. Two very important things came out. One was the ability to communicate. We have excellent communication skills among ourselves. Communication didn't start when they started in the business. It started when they were 4 or 5 at the breakfast table or basketball court. We try to have dinner together every night. Every Sunday we would go to church. I think that strengthened family values. My wife is great. She's the chief emotional officer. When you give people security and enough love to go around and respect them, they are secure. When people are anxious or nervous or worried, they are that way because they're not given enough love.

Those values were transmitted to the children. My wife and I insisted on excellence in education. I guess if we had had a child that didn't want to study we would have had to force them. But we really tried to mold them to do well in school. They went to the best schools here but every summer we sent them to the U.S. for summer programs. Since my grandfather never had an opportunity to have a good education, he used to tell me 'I told your father that I'm not going to give him that inheritance from me. The only thing I'm going to leave him and your uncles and aunts is an education. That's the only inheritance that no one can take away from you.' That was a very nice message.

He helped his children see that despite living in a highly affluent community, they would not have everything other kids had. While they were richer than most of their peer families, his children were taught to be thoughtful about their spending.

Young children learn about work by doing chores and helping around the house. If there is a family business or family office, they may experience work by helping there. This may also be the first time they get paid. By visiting the family business and seeing how work is done, they directly view the source of the family legacy, and imagine their own possible future. Similarly, if a family engages together in community service work, children learn about other cultures and the challenges of a world where some have and others do not. This is a difficult moral lesson.

"We know what a drug money can be as it stopped children from becoming the best they could be. I didn't want that for our children," says a matriarch of one branch of a large many-generation family. "I was very conscious that I wanted my children to make it on their own." This desire in turn led her and her husband to work actively with their own family branch, developing a strong family organization to introduce a contrasting culture of excellence for her children.

WISE COUNSEL RESEARCH
44 WINDSOR ROAD
MILTON, MA 02186

DENNIS T. JAFFE, PH.D.
DENNIS@WISECOUNSELRESEARCH.COM
WWW. WISECOUNSELRESEARCH.COM

RELEASING THE POTENTIAL OF THE RISING GENERATION:

Sharing family values and discussion about money and wealth is a critical task for a wealthy family. One South American family heir reports how the family established a "counter culture" that challenged the prevailing materialism seen in their peers, a difficult lesson for them to learn:

I noticed a lot of children are given polo lessons, yachts, sports cars very early. We have stayed away from that. The first car they got was a Volvo. No yachts, no polo. It's about work and helping your neighbor, loving your family. When our friends at school would get something like a fancy new bike, my mother would say 'well, that's not necessary. You can have a simple bicycle. It will do the same thing.' They never tried to match up to the advantages of other people. So if somebody had a car, we had a bicycle. Or if somebody had Nike we had Converse. In that sense, money was not important. It was never discussed until we were older. We learned to be moderate with money, have control over it. Don't overextend yourself.

I remember I had a savings box made out of paper mache. Every day they gave us 75 cents or a dollar to buy a coke or candy. I never bought the coke or candy. I saved the money and put it in my savings box every day for I don't know how many years. I saved almost $2,000 like that. Then I bought stocks. I was about 14 or 15 and I said to my dad 'why don't you buy some stocks for me?' So he bought me some stock that I still have. I also collected auto stickers and sold them at school. With that money I bought a croquet game with my neighbors and we formed a croquet league.

One challenge of longstanding family wealth is a by-product of its success. Over generations, the family establishes a public image of values and service to the community, as well as a vibrant and successful business. The outside view is of prosperity and service. The next generation family members benefit from this perception by experiencing respect and community status, but also sometimes envy and jealousy.

Young family members may need help to respond to this public perception:

In terms of values I keep stressing why we want to stay together. Very few people in my family have anybody to relate to with this wealth other than ourselves. We're not the Rockefellers. We all live with the fact that people assume that we have private jets and live this grand life, which we don't. But we're much better off than most of our friends so we're very fortunate. Nobody wants to complain about having money or the issues that come with it so there is a big void of how you discuss this or who you discuss it with. By getting together we earn a comfort zone that we can talk about it. We need to rely on each other that way. Share experiences, thoughts. How do we deal with that as it goes to our kids? We all are guinea pigs.

While the "family" is wealthy, individual members may have no control or access to that wealth. This may make them uncertain and uncomfortable. How do they react when someone asks for a loan or expects them to always pick up the check at dinner? Several heirs mentioned the importance of not having their family wealth known to their peers; one family member changed his name when he entered college so that he would not be associated with his parents' donations.

Families all over the world share one quality in relation to wealth: they usually don't talk about it, or do so with great difficulty. Every legacy family had to experience the distrust and incapacity that came from keeping it secret from their children, and to learn (often after a struggle) how to talk with them about money, wealth and inheritance. Rarely does a family do this from the start. A second or third generation leader,

WISE COUNSEL RESEARCH
44 WINDSOR ROAD
MILTON, MA 02186

DENNIS T. JAFFE, PH.D.
DENNIS@WISECOUNSELRESEARCH.COM
WWW. WISECOUNSELRESEARCH.COM

HOW LONG-LASTING FAMILY ENTERPRISES PREPARE THEIR SUCCESSORS

non-family leader or advisor, can guide the family to this conversation. We heard how one family had difficulty with their first attempt at a family discussion. But they tried again, and were more successful.

If the family does not allow their children to talk about money and wealth, their feelings and struggle will have no outlet, and they may make self-defeating life choices. Several family members talked about feeling a vague sense of guilt about having money. "I didn't earn it, so I didn't feel it was really mine." While providing many benefits, members of wealthy families are always aware of the double-edged nature of inherited wealth. Young people need guidance to deal with these mixed feelings, and this guidance is best delivered in personal discussions.

Generative families learn to meet regularly to talk money and wealth, in strong contrast to most families, even affluent ones, who do not talk about this. Parents in legacy families recall conversations about the future. They try to take a light touch, making it possible for the next generation to become involved, but also establishing clear values and expectations for them.

3

The 24-Hour Family "How are You" Meeting

Explaining the meaning and use of family wealth is difficult. It demands a high level of engagement and give and take. Here is a creative example from a European family patriarch who holds regular meetings with his two sons who work with him in the business:

It's still small enough to do that on an informal basis but we realize that in the future that's going to have to be more formal. Me and my sons (the third to fourth generation) have over the last 10 years formalized meetings about transition. Twice a year we sit together for 24 hours. We call this the 'how are you meeting.' We exchange views of what kind of things we are going to work on for the next generation in a formal way. It's like a business family meeting. We do it here in my house.

The basic question is: how are things going in general, what are the top preoccupations in your head? What can make the other parties happier. We look at what do you like and what you don't like, what went wrong or what can I do to make you happier? I make mistakes and you make mistakes and you are going to do that every week, and you have to accept the way you are. You cannot change that, but it's good that you know that so you will try to avoid these negative things.

What causes parents and children to start talking? It could be a crisis, a sudden or untimely death or a financial windfall or loss. Or it can be a question voiced by a young family member. The parent can either open up or shut down the conversation.

It is difficult for parents and young children to talk freely and candidly. One reason is that young people feel that their parents are looking for specific responses and have a hidden purpose in what they are asking. So, in order to have family conversation, to convey that they are open to hearing what their children think, a parent has to ask more questions than state their opinions. A parent has to make it clear they want to hear the answer and not interrupt. If they get a one-word answer, they gently probe by asking further questions. This is called "having an attitude of inquiry rather than advocacy". While a parent does in fact have an agenda and opinions, waiting to learn from the young person what they think and feel first, is a path to a successful family conversation.

WISE COUNSEL RESEARCH
44 WINDSOR ROAD
MILTON, MA 02186

DENNIS T. JAFFE, PH.D.
DENNIS@WISECOUNSELRESEARCH.COM
WWW. WISECOUNSELRESEARCH.COM

RELEASING THE POTENTIAL OF THE RISING GENERATION:

Values Conversations

Instilling values is rarely a formal process. Rather, through their own actions parents set an example. However, several legacy families also initiated conversations with their children specifically about the meaning of family wealth. There seems to be no set age for doing this. Most families adopted a graduated method of conversation—sharing information and teaching skills at different ages as appropriate. "We've talked about where happiness comes from, having a good solid family, good solid friends, good food, a happy life at school. Things that are very tangible that you can call on all the time," said an inheritor who is now chair of her family's council.

Most families who have been successful over multiple generations develop an ethic of thoughtful spending, setting limits on how much the family spends in an external environment that enshrines consumption. It takes the concerted effort of a parent to instill this sensitivity. This 6th generation family, with a long history in several countries, embodies the following values:

> Our values are focused on trying to live in a frugal way, trying not to abuse family wealth and respect other people. We're distributing relatively modest amounts at a relatively young age. I've heard of other families where at age 18, they come into a trust fund where they're rolling in millions of dollars. It's important for us not to do that because that way, you're causing major issues for future generations.

4

Desired Values for Successors

Surprisingly, we found that the values legacy families desire for their children are remarkably similar in every part of the world:

- **Generosity:** give back to the community

- **Respect:** for people of all wealth backgrounds

- **A strong work ethic and skills:** capability to earn their own money and to find work they care about and at which they can succeed

- **Self-esteem:** independent of their wealth

- **Financial literacy:** learn how to handle money

- **Responsibility for wealth:** not being spoiled by affluence. Understand that it is a tool not an end in itself

- **Frugality and prudence about spending**

- **Pride and appreciation for the opportunity wealth offers**

The efforts we describe here are largely aimed at creating a family climate for these values to emerge.

WISE COUNSEL RESEARCH
44 WINDSOR ROAD
MILTON, MA 02186

DENNIS T. JAFFE, PH.D.
DENNIS@WISECOUNSELRESEARCH.COM
WWW. WISECOUNSELRESEARCH.COM

HOW LONG-LASTING FAMILY ENTERPRISES PREPARE THEIR SUCCESSORS

The founding generation's values are influential, as a third generation family leader of a European family states:

The dividends are not something we've actually earned. Prior generations put together this company and did a lot of hard work so we need to be responsible and wise with the money that we are given, not live extravagantly. We give a lot philanthropically and live modestly, like my grandfather and grandmother who created the company. They chose to live in the same one story brick house they've lived in for 50 years rather than deciding to upgrade to some kind of extravagant mansion. They were happy and content and satisfied with what they had and spend their money in other ways whether it would be taking family and friends on trips to places or cultural things. There is an overriding mentality to not take for granted what you have and use it for education and long-term value.

Grandparents (elders) can be powerful teachers and models. Their special relationship with their grandchildren and their venerated history, allow them to share their special family legacy:

We get together each summer for two weeks without the parents; it's our opportunity as grandparents to give back to the next generation some of our values, pass along some of our traditions and to nurture that history and those traditions. Every five years our family has an important ceremony. We dress up. It starts at age five when the child is five years old; we plant a tree for them at our country house. At age 10 they get the treasure chest, filled with all of the history of the family and the DVDs and all the artifacts.

5

The Three-Box Tool for Teaching Money Values

Values education begins early at home. One tool mentioned by several families is the "three boxes." When a child is first given an allowance, they are asked to allocate the money into three boxes: one for spending, one for saving, and one for giving away. This distinction is difficult for a young child to understand at first, but, once learned, the principle will have lasting impact on their lives. Here is one parent's account of adopting this activity and its impact:

Our kids have been raised in a household that embodied, 'to whom much is given much is expected,' has been modeled. We began when they were probably four years old, they got an allowance and had a spend jar, a saving jar and a giving jar. They had to cut it in thirds and put it in each of those jars. Then through school activities, church and other things, they began giving their giving jar money at a very early age. Over the years whenever we have made a significant contribution we ask the family to come together. They have attended numerous philanthropic events and functions. We have a governance agreement that you can't come to the company until you work two years outside of the company. When he finished college my son went to work for Teach for America and supported intercity kids in very difficult circumstances.

Here is another:

A lot of people wonder, 'Well, my kid's only 10 now. There's no need to teach him anything until he's 18, right?' But I think the real answer goes right back to when they're age four or five. We latched onto the three piggy bank idea. We give the kids an allowance each week, but they have to remember to ask for it, which is a little twist that not many people do. They actually have some responsibility to ask for it and remember,

WISE COUNSEL RESEARCH
44 WINDSOR ROAD
MILTON, MA 02186

DENNIS T. JAFFE, PH.D.
DENNIS@WISECOUNSELRESEARCH.COM
WWW. WISECOUNSELRESEARCH.COM

RELEASING THE POTENTIAL OF THE RISING GENERATION:

so that it's not like a dividend check that just shows up every year. We give them three coins and they've got three piggy banks. One's got 'spending' written on it, one's got 'saving' written on it, one's got 'charity' written on it. Each week, they put a coin in each one. That leads to great learning opportunities and teaching moments. So if there's a bushfire on TV or something and the kids think that that's bad that somebody's house got burned down, then we say, 'Let's use some of the money in your charity piggy bank and put it towards people that they're going to help.' They go to their piggy bank and see they've got $10 in there. Then there's a decision on how much give. 'If you give it all to this one, you don't have no more for any others'. They can start to think about all these different issues when they're really young, and it comes naturally to them.

They learn the value of money. Some of my kids' friends don't know whether a car costs $1,000 or $1 million. But in their spending piggy bank, if they've got a certain amount of money in there, then when you're in a shop and the kids are always saying, 'I want this Lego,' or, 'I want that toy.' The discussion can come back to, 'Well, how much do you have in your spending piggybank?' 'Oh, I've got $10.' Well then, that $50 Lego box doesn't look so good then, does it, if you have to buy it?

My kids spontaneously decided to set up a store on the curb, selling anything they can get their hands on, whether it's rocks from the garden or flowers or palm fronds or paper planes or whatever they can do. They set up a sign and say it's for charity and stop people in the street. They've made a surprising amount of money. They enjoy doing it, putting the time in. And then we have a great discussion about, 'Okay, how will we spend it?' With some charities, you can say, 'Well, you can buy a sheep for one family or you could buy 20 chickens or you can buy fruit trees.' Then you have a discussion about what will last longer, what's most beneficial, all these things. It all leads to great discussion, and I'm hoping it becomes embedded in the kids from a really early age.

Learning About Business and Work

Families usually expect and require family members to work. None of the families in this study desired non-working family members. But the definition of work was flexible, "We have a requirement for work but we don't have a requirement for a salary so if someone chooses their life work to be a volunteer coordinator for some charity we consider that employment. We would consider that work."

Another family developed what they call "the Passion Project" where each young family member was invited to develop a business, funded by the family, doing something they were passionate about, where they had demonstrated persistence and commitment, that was recognized in some way by the relevant community. These projects were not necessarily remunerative; the family supported arts or social service projects if the receiver demonstrated its worth to the community.

Education about the family business happens informally and is important in developing expectations and focusing on career goals. This Middle Eastern family member, with widely dispersed family members, remembers:

I was just dragged to meetings since I was five or six. If there was a meeting on the weekend or I was on holiday I would just get dragged along. So that was one way. Second there were always business guests at home. There were always family members staying at a home, nephews or uncles or people visiting for

WISE COUNSEL RESEARCH
44 WINDSOR ROAD
MILTON, MA 02186

DENNIS T. JAFFE, PH.D.
DENNIS@WISECOUNSELRESEARCH.COM
WWW. WISECOUNSELRESEARCH.COM

HOW LONG-LASTING FAMILY ENTERPRISES PREPARE THEIR SUCCESSORS

business. We lived with my grandfather, so there was always conversation between my father and my grandfather or my father and his brothers that were visiting. You couldn't help but hear although you didn't always understand it until later on. You heard and were involved passively.

Wealth opens up special opportunities for the rising generation to pursue rewarding career directions not open to less fortunate families. A family elder noticing the musical talent shown by a young family member, without her knowledge asked the trust to invest in a rare instrument that was being auctioned. It was a good investment in a valuable antique and also a way to support a special talent. The young family member has gone on to teach and play all over the world. Other families reported that they invest in the human capital of family members, when they show special motivation or ability.

6

Developing a Positive Work Ethic
Here is an account by a third generation father about developing work values:

My older sister was born in a small apartment. I was born in a nice house. Then my younger sister spent her formative years were in a much nicer house. All of us saw an incredible work ethic from my dad and uncle. A big challenge for me is how does my kid know how hard I'm working?

I knew clearly that my dad busted his ass. He was gone from six in the morning until ten at night six days a week. Sunday he'd sleep in until seven or eight. He made it to my games, but on the other hand I knew what he was doing. One of the benefits of working in the family office is that I can take my kid to school everyday. I don't miss a game. How does my kid see that work ethic? That's one of the struggles my dad never had. He just did it. My generation hopefully will struggle with that and hopefully have good answers so the next generation is more comfortable with their wealth. Not that we're uncomfortable but I think we're just learning how to do it. My dad couldn't teach me how to be born into wealth.

Family members have to rely on each other, to teach them the values that need to go with it. The reason my generation struggles with it is because we saw it, we lived it, now it's ours. I've got to figure out how to make sure that my kids have a strong work ethic or understand the value of money. I went from a six figure marketing job to teaching high school for $28,000 bucks yet still living the lifestyle of a six figure marketing guy in Manhattan. That's not a reality for most people. How do you bridge that gap and let a kid understand? It's important that we educate our kids and rely on each other. That's where the family comes in. I see as my responsibility for my niece who might not be getting that idea. I have to step in somehow because I think their mother is doing a poor job of it.

Several parents noted that they were especially active when their children transitioned from university to their first work experience. With the cushion of family wealth, a young person looking forward to inheriting or working in the family business may have lower motivation to struggle and learn from adversity in their early work efforts. Indeed, adversity may be a new experience:

Their parents help them through those critical stages; the end of school and through university in their first years post-university. I think their critical stage is that first post-university job. They'd better start somewhere although it's not easy or pleasant. Both our daughters had first jobs at interesting companies but with terrible bosses. They learned really good lessons about life in the real world. They didn't stay very long with those

WISE COUNSEL RESEARCH
44 WINDSOR ROAD
MILTON, MA 02186

DENNIS T. JAFFE, PH.D.
DENNIS@WISECOUNSELRESEARCH.COM
WWW. WISECOUNSELRESEARCH.COM

RELEASING THE POTENTIAL OF THE RISING GENERATION:

jobs but when you're starting out, you've got to get your hands dirty and start at the bottom. But some family members think, 'I don't need to do it. I can sort of skip' that first phase out of university. But I just don't think you can. I didn't. I started working in a public works project as a young graduate engineer. The transition from university where it's still partying and fun, to the real world where you often start with a pretty crummy job. They're going to start with a pretty basic job that's not going to pay them very well.

One second generation elder summed up his generation's work with the following vision for the next generation:

I wish the next generation can see what we are and where we've come from merely as a background to who they will become. There is no sense of entitlement to either position or income. I hope they see it as part of their roots, something they're pleased about. And we'll give a little bit of time and intellectual bandwidth so they can be effective shareholders and owners. I don't want to look beyond that generation. Who knows what might happen; I'm not particularly dynastic. It was up to my generation to do the rational things when we crystallize the wealth. And in due course, it will be the opportunity for the next generation.

I want them to be able to function as a unit that enables them to avoid defaulting to 'let's stop doing this because we don't know each other and can't work together, but let's make an informed decision about where we're going now as a family group.' I do think that there's value in that just because it's nice to know where you come from as an individual and as a family. There's a sense of identity and connection that gives people a good foundation to live their lives with knowledge about where it's come from. I always say we're not special. We just got lucky. If you're lucky then what measures your success is how you capitalize on luck. In other words, be the best you can then don't sit around. The disease of the inheritor, we all know, is the propensity to undershoot their potential because the inherited capital allows them to do that. Most humans are pretty lazy. I hope that would only be the minority of cases in this family, that they'll just get on and enjoy life and live life to the full. We don't need to go 10 generations. We just need to do a good job each generation and see what happens.

DEVELOPING IDENTITY AS A CHILD OF WEALTH[6]

Even with parental support and engagement, a young person growing up in a wealthy household must develop a positive identity independent of the family, while also defining careers, lives and desired adult relationship to the family. While there are many examples of materialistic, entitled, "spoiled," even self-destructive and lost young people, the stories of families in our study convinces us that an engaged, values-based investment in the next generation by the elders of the family is a strong antidote to this tendency. It begins in the household and then expands to the extended family "community" of cousins growing up in the shadow of the family enterprise. The extended family reinforces the message by offering membership in a wonderful community that shares a business and commitment to positive social values. Membership has rewards but is also a responsibility. To prepare to join the extended family, the young person first embarks

---

6 The observation that it is difficult to grow up in a wealthy household and to develop a positive identity is an insight that comes from a group of researchers including John Levy, Joanie Bronfman, Joline Godfrey, Lee Hausner, Jim Grubman, David Bork and Madeline Levine, who have each written extensively on this topic.

WISE COUNSEL RESEARCH
44 WINDSOR ROAD
MILTON, MA 02186

DENNIS T. JAFFE, PH.D.
DENNIS@WISECOUNSELRESEARCH.COM
WWW. WISECOUNSELRESEARCH.COM

HOW LONG-LASTING FAMILY ENTERPRISES PREPARE THEIR SUCCESSORS

on a journey to develop a personal sense of purpose and capability that in turn enables a positive role in the family enterprise.

Growing up in a wealthy household, the trappings of wealth are omnipresent. This reinforces a sense that they are "special" in undefined ways, affecting expectations, questions and concerns about their future. This upbringing potentially provides inheritors an unusual amount of freedom to define themselves. But this same freedom and privilege also challenges how to make good choices and feel good about their fortune in a world where people with inherited wealth may feel devalued by others who have less and resent them. The way a young inheritor integrates the presence of money and wealth into his or her work, personal relationships and life choices, creates 'wealth identity'[7].

Knowing their life is subsidized, how do they motivate themselves among so many possibilities and choose what to do with their lives? Living in the outsize shadows of their parents, they wonder what they can do that will be significant and important. The opportunities of wealth can be lost if spent on meaningless, self-defeating or destructive pursuits. It can be a source of confusion if inheritors are not sure what it means to them, what they want to do with it, or how it fits into their lives. They find themselves doing a little of this, a little of that, and not having enough motivation to stick with anything.

Money alone is not the issue. It is also the status and recognition that comes with wealth, potentially leading to feelings of power and entitlement but also feelings of entrapment and isolation. Having and inheriting money has a marked impact on one's core identity — on the beliefs and values that map how they view themselves as well as how others see them. Inheritors can experience guilt or feel that they do not deserve these gifts, complicating their ability to move forward with a positive relationship to their wealth. After learning from their parents, they have to work on their own to develop their own personal identity. Identity development does not emerge fully from parents' teaching. However, the experience of being part of an extended family community can aid their journey immeasurably.

Wealthy heirs nowadays grow up in a bubble, a "gilded ghetto"[8] where they mostly meet others like themselves. Being protected they do not experience diversity or have much opportunity to manage their own affairs. They do not go out or even play on their own. With all of their wealth, their life experience is limited. Entering college may be one of the first times they are on their own, sharing space and getting places on time without reminders. They may meet and learn from people different than them and expand their horizons, or remain secluded within a tight circle of other heirs. They need to be prepared and encouraged to take the first path.

Several family practices help young people navigate this path. First, the elders let go and allow young adults to find their way. They should be encouraged to set out on their own, with appropriate support for things like education or travel, but not so much that they don't have to do some things for themselves. What they can expect should be made explicit, and parents should try as much as they can not to give mixed messages that show disapproval of their choices. This can be tough for parents who feel strongly about certain directions.

---

7 Goldbart, S., Jaffe, D. and DiFuria, J. (2004). *Money, Meaning and Identity: Coming to Terms with Being Wealthy*. From **Psychology and Consumer Culture**. T. Kasser and A. Kanner, eds. American Psychological Association.

8 O'Neal, Jessie. (1997). **The Golden Ghetto**. The Affluenza Project.

WISE COUNSEL RESEARCH
44 WINDSOR ROAD
MILTON, MA 02186

DENNIS T. JAFFE, PH.D.
DENNIS@WISECOUNSELRESEARCH.COM
WWW. WISECOUNSELRESEARCH.COM

RELEASING THE POTENTIAL OF THE RISING GENERATION:

Young people want their families to be interested and supportive of what they do, withholding criticism and control over their choices. In this life stage parents can be appreciative, but no longer in control. Parents should resist their desire to use money to control choices and behavior. Young people develop best when they feel that while there are resources behind them, they are also expected to be on their own, even self-supporting. The family should have a clear agreement about what can be expected and what they are expected to do. The presence of trusts and money is a problem if the rules for what is theirs and what is not are unclear.

Many young people report difficult experiences that lead them to learn and grow. If they don't struggle, they cannot learn. So, parents who are rescuers, or who support them in avoiding the consequences of difficulties, prevent learning. When a crisis or difficulty leads the young person to learn and grow, a common developmental sequence of identity development emerges that follows the lines of the Hero's Journey[9]—a person sets out to find something, encounters setbacks and difficulties, and overcomes them with some help from outside, to end up with the prize of a sense of personal identity and meaning. Identity development can be viewed as a personal journey of difficult lessons and obstacles overcome, leading to public achievement and recognition as they return home.

Young people who grow up with wealth inhabit a state of innocence[10]—where they feel special and powerful, that nothing can happen to them. Then something happens—a personal failure, a difficult relationship, or a challenge—that signals they can't rely on their parents or their money, but have to do something on their own. They are hurt and troubled, and this sets them to learn, reflect and come to terms with what they want to do with their lives. They may have to overcome bad habits or personal difficulties. They develop on their own some of the confidence, self-acceptance and sense of purpose of their parents.

For parents, anxiety and desire for the best for their children can lead to rescuing them from any nascent difficulty, leading to a cycle of co-dependency where the child knows that parents will always be there to take care of them. Parents who find their young adult children in trouble or hurting have to be able to apply positive tough love—emotional support along with the message that they have to solve their problems without unlimited parental resources. This lesson must first be learned by the parent.

Parental engagement is tricky at this stage. A parent should find a way to be in regular contact, as a sounding board for some (not all) experiences, but taking care to be supportive and ask questions rather than preach or tell what to do. Support does not have to mean solving a problem or intervening. Using one's means to smooth a path in college or a job is almost always counter-productive. For a parent used to having direct impact and taking action, this stage of support can be difficult to learn. They are not used to such an indirect role.

---

9 This concept, by mythologist Joseph Campbell, suggests that over a life, a young person often follows a common developmental journey told in different ways across cultures, which contains a quest, a setting out, facing a deep challenge and danger, finding allies and overcoming it, to return home as a hero.

10 A term coined by George Kinder. (1999) in **Seven Stages of Money Maturity**, Dell, to denote those who enjoy wealth but have no idea where it comes from or how to manage it.

WISE COUNSEL RESEARCH
44 WINDSOR ROAD
MILTON, MA 02186

DENNIS T. JAFFE, PH.D.
DENNIS@WISECOUNSELRESEARCH.COM
WWW. WISECOUNSELRESEARCH.COM

HOW LONG-LASTING FAMILY ENTERPRISES PREPARE THEIR SUCCESSORS

The young person who emerges from his or her own journey, develops a sense of self strong enough to be ready to become involved in family ventures. They return home with their own success at doing something well, and a set of skills they are ready to offer to the family.

WISE COUNSEL RESEARCH
44 WINDSOR ROAD
MILTON, MA 02186

DENNIS T. JAFFE, PH.D.
DENNIS@WISECOUNSELRESEARCH.COM
WWW. WISECOUNSELRESEARCH.COM

RELEASING THE POTENTIAL OF THE RISING GENERATION:

GUEST COMMENTARY

"WHY FLYING COACH DOESN'T MATTER (AND WHAT DOES)"
Madeline Levine, Ph.D.

The most frequent concern that wealthy parents have about their children is that they will be spoiled or entitled. They worry that their children will not appreciate the value of hard work. That they will conflate their parents' wealth and stature with their own. That, after a childhood of privilege and ease, they will expect that the world owes them a living. Parents worry that while their childrens' bank accounts may be robust; their identities may be pitifully thin. They want to know how to avoid these kind of unfortunate outcomes. While all kinds of factors, including genetics, go into the construction of a young adult, parenting is the only thing we have control over. That control needs to be exercised thoughtfully and with an eye towards the kind of values that every parent hopes to inculcate in children.

So what matters when it comes to raising good kids in the unusual circumstance of great wealth? Consider these two examples:

- Seventeen-year-old Carey, an only child, is forced by her concerned and wealth ambivalent mother, to fly commercial coach even when her parents are flying either first class, or more often, on their own plane. Mom believes that Carey "has to see that most people are not as privileged as she is." For her part Carey is expectedly angry and unfortunately rude. She feels punished by the fact that her parents are wealthy and treats both her seatmate and the flight attendants with contempt. Mom drags her into my office worried about her haughty behavior.

- Nineteen-year-old Ty has been taking flying lessons for several years. He has a deep interest in aviation and at the moment thinks he is more likely to pursue a degree in aviation engineering than in business. When the family flies private he flies with them. He is polite and thankful to all and engages in spirited conversations with the pilot about aviation history and mechanics. Mom wants to know if she should have him fly commercial "a few times" to gain a better appreciation of how most people travel.

The issue of how children should fly comes up so often when dealing with extremely wealthy families that it has become a kind of metaphor for both the privilege of wealth and the concern that wealth will diminish a child's character and appreciation of the "real world." In my opinion, it is an incidental, even trivial concern that masks far more significant issues that trouble parents. How will my child appreciate the privilege they have? How can I expose them to the realities of life outside of "the bubble" in which they live? How do I help my children steer clear of a sense of entitlement? How do I make sure that they grow into good, healthy people who know themselves and can conduct themselves well in contexts other than wealth?

Let's think about the flying concern as a symptom and the concerns about values, integrity and identity as the root causes. People typically want relief from a troubling symptom so let's attend to that quickly. Ultra wealthy people often have their own planes. From a psychologists point of view, the decision about whether a child should fly private, first class or coach begs the question of what kind of child is doing the flying and how parents feel about their own good fortune. If like Carey, the child is entitled and angry (unfortunate but understandable given her exclusion from the family) then where she sits on a plane should be the least of her parents concerns. Children do not learn good values by punishment; they learn to be good by watching the behavior of the people closest to them.

WISE COUNSEL RESEARCH
44 WINDSOR ROAD
MILTON, MA 02186

DENNIS T. JAFFE, PH.D.
DENNIS@WISECOUNSELRESEARCH.COM
WWW. WISECOUNSELRESEARCH.COM

HOW LONG-LASTING FAMILY ENTERPRISES PREPARE THEIR SUCCESSORS

Ty has learned his good manners by watching parents who are not ambivalent about their wealth, but who are grateful for it. He learned to thank the pilot and the attendant by watching his parents, by their expectation that he would respond similarly and by their respect for his interest in aviation (a far cry from the family business in hatcheries.) Flying privately has helped Ty to learn how to be a respectful participant in a wealthy family and has given him the opportunity to deeply explore an interest that may well become part of his identity. Carey, on the other hand, has primarily learned that wealth is a problem that needs corrective actions. Her experiences are unlikely to achieve the results that her parents hope for.

Great wealth does provide the opportunity for extraordinary experiences. Children should not be made to feel guilty about these experiences. Nor should parents (unless extraordinary experiences become an apology for neglect.) Child development proceeds in a more or less predictable fashion. Self-control, interpersonal skills, engagement, integrity and identity are stages of development that need successful resolution regardless of socio-economic status. For children who come from families of great wealth, the resolution of these stages has implications both for the child him or herself, but also for the family business, the family enterprise and the larger community. Here are some of the better known ways of encouraging healthy moral development and a robust sense of self in children. This process doesn't end at any particular age. Science now tells us that the brain keeps developing well into a child's 20's. It's never too late.

1. **Model the behavior you want to see in your children.** They watch you far more intently than they listen to you. Make sure that you treat people around you with respect and interest. Expect your child to do the same. Always have them thank people who have helped them. Make it a habit.

2. **Insist that your children have chores.** The fact that someone makes your bed doesn't mean that your child doesn't need to learn how to make a bed. Their college roommate or future spouse will thank you. Being independent and able to take care of oneself feeds confidence, resilience and identity. When they become teenagers have them take a "regular" job, not a cushy one at the family office. Have them stand on their feet. Nothing encourages empathy like experience.

3. **Work on clearing up your own feelings about wealth.** If you are ambivalent or feel that it is primarily burdensome, then your kids are likely to be, at best confused, at worst angry and rebellious. Kids do well when their parents do well. Put your own mask on first.

4. **Bring them into the philanthropic process earlier rather than later.** Make it a given from early on that part of the family culture is "giving back." By age 9 or 10, but certainly by early adolescence, kids can begin learning both leadership skills and the skills needed to evaluate philanthropic ventures. Start off small. Teach and guide. Make it a family project.

5. **Allow a period of time that is free from the concerns of the family business or enterprise.** Developing a strong sense of identity is a full-time job. Pair it with becoming educated and kids have an awful lot on their plate. Give them a breather. College can be a good time for this.

6. **Practice gratitude.** Hands around the dinner table. Church or synagogue. Commitment to some cause. Don't just say how grateful you are. Prove it.

Madeline Levine, PhD is a psychologist with close to 30 years of experience as a clinician, educator and author, with two New York Times best sellers, The Price of Privilege *and* Teach Your Children Well. *She is also co-founder of Challenge Success a program of the Stanford University Graduate School of Education.*

WISE COUNSEL RESEARCH
44 WINDSOR ROAD
MILTON, MA 02186

DENNIS T. JAFFE, PH.D.
DENNIS@WISECOUNSELRESEARCH.COM
WWW. WISECOUNSELRESEARCH.COM

RELEASING THE POTENTIAL OF THE RISING GENERATION:

APPLYING WHAT YOU LEARNED: QUESTIONS FOR FAMILY REFLECTION.

These questions can be posed to family members to begin a conversation related to the key ideas presented in Part Two.

For the Parents:	For the Rising Generation:
• What messages about money and wealth do you want to pass to your children?	• What values did you learn from your family about money and wealth?
• How do you talk to your children about the family wealth and how special it is to have it?	• How does the presence of family wealth affect your life choices and future?
• What values do you want your children to develop, and how have you consciously helped make this happen?	• What are you doing to prepare for your life and career?
• What are the messages that you have to help your children set off on their own life journey when they finish their education (or before)?	• What help and support do you need from your family?
	• In what ways are you considering becoming involved in family activities having to do with the family enterprises?

WISE COUNSEL RESEARCH
44 WINDSOR ROAD
MILTON, MA 02186

DENNIS T. JAFFE, PH.D.
DENNIS@WISECOUNSELRESEARCH.COM
WWW. WISECOUNSELRESEARCH.COM

HOW LONG-LASTING FAMILY ENTERPRISES PREPARE THEIR SUCCESSORS

PART III: THE FAMILY COMMUNITY AS A LEARNING SYSTEM

Consider a young third generation family member from a wealthy and successful family. She grew up barely knowing her cousins who lived in different cities. She is proud of the business that bears her mother's maiden name, but neither her cousins nor the family business are a day-to-day reality for her. Her parents and siblings are her anchors, and she has not seriously considered any specific role in the family enterprise. Not that she isn't interested; it's just not on her radar.

When she is about to start high school, the extended family holds the first of what becomes an annual family retreat. She spends fun time with her cousins and discovers how much she has in common with them. Upon learning the history of their legacy business and the role of the new family office, she has the notion that perhaps she might study business and eventually have a role in sales and marketing. She takes a mini-course with her cousins about budgeting, household expenses, and using credit cards, topics she had never thought about as her parents paid for everything. She loves the summer meetings and volunteers to join the committee to plan next year's meeting. This is how a third generation family initiates the opportunity for the next generation to become a legacy family.

The success of a new generation in a family enterprise begins with self-awareness not just of a group of related families but a **community** with shared values, organization and collective activities. While they are relatives, they are not really a united family until they decide to become one, and actively pursue that goal. A clear impression from our research is that a generative family succeeds across generations when it creates an extensive family organization and educational activities that guide the rising generation into active roles as leaders and stewards of the family "capitals." These family communities sustain legacy family values and resources, but also take them in new directions. This section does not pretend to do justice to these many family activities; we focus on those related to family development and education.[11]

Education and development for the rising generation is a dual responsibility of the individual household and the extended family. First, as we have seen, comes informal learning within the individual household. Due to the scale and complexity of the needs and responsibilities of the large family enterprise, more guidance is needed. Hence, by the third generation, the extended family takes up the task of creating shared efforts, coordinated by a self-initiating group of family members who form an education committee or task force, usually growing out of (or sometimes into) the family council.[12]

While members can be appointed to this committee, no one can appoint commitment. Most families encourage a few family members to volunteer and step up. The education committee usually contains members of more than one generation. Its primary tasks are creating curriculum, employing resources, finding places and getting family members to attend. Families make use of outside advisors, and frequently call upon family office executives to help. Some families pay a family member to act as the coordinator of their educational programs.

---

11 Future working papers will present the topics of governance, business renewal, creating family connection, and philanthropy.

12 The family council is one of the unique creations of family governance that distinguishes the generative family. A full account of family councils, that coordinate the tasks of the family to oversee the business, build personal connection and develop the next generation, will be the topic of our next working paper.

WISE COUNSEL RESEARCH
44 WINDSOR ROAD
MILTON, MA 02186

DENNIS T. JAFFE, PH.D.
DENNIS@WISECOUNSELRESEARCH.COM
WWW. WISECOUNSELRESEARCH.COM

RELEASING THE POTENTIAL OF THE RISING GENERATION:

As they enter G3, several of the most successful legacy families—having upwards of 50 people in the emerging generation—create a portfolio of next generation activities. As households begin to disperse and children grow up further from the direct experience of what the family does, generative families actively create opportunities to build connection. These often take the form of annual gatherings that:

- Develop or strengthen a sense of family,

- Enable young people to get to know each other, and

- Inform the emerging generation about the family history and its business.

These retreats can be very elaborate (and costly!). Generative families report that they made a conscious choice to invest in the development of family.

These extended family activities include the following, which we will describe more fully below:

- **Cross-Generational Community Meetings**

- **Business/Financial Briefings**

- **Educational Programs**

- **Mentoring and Career Development**

CROSS-GENERATIONAL COMMUNITY MEETINGS

Relationship building and education begins when the extended family meets together to define themselves as a shared community of interest. By the third generation, the legacy family contains branches, households, and dispersed family members that do not know each other well. From a group of related kin, they must generate an active desire to be together, and a common identity concerning who they are and what they are doing together. Otherwise, forces of separation will overcome their shared legacy as a financial entity.

Building extended family relationships often begins with summer gatherings for young people and teenagers:

Because they live all over the place, we have a gathering every summer for the teenagers. This last summer was our third year, so we had a whole family reunion. The summer before that, my daughter and her husband who are in the fourth generation, hosted the teen reunion at our family cabin. We had 15 teenagers show up. I was the cook, stayed all the way. Even living all over the place, they're instantly friends.

How can these simple gatherings become so consequential as to lead to the development of a legacy family? Members of the rising generation meet and get to know each other. They discover how much their shared legacy draws them together. They then consider whether they want to work together in the future, and perhaps get excited about future possibilities that build upon their legacy. Out of their growing sense of connection and community, they initiate leadership and engage the older generation in their ideas for the future.

WISE COUNSEL RESEARCH
44 WINDSOR ROAD
MILTON, MA 02186

DENNIS T. JAFFE, PH.D.
DENNIS@WISECOUNSELRESEARCH.COM
WWW. WISECOUNSELRESEARCH.COM

HOW LONG-LASTING FAMILY ENTERPRISES PREPARE THEIR SUCCESSORS

At the turn of the 20th century, wealthy US families often developed family summer encampments, a special place for the whole family to gather. Many legacy families today maintain this tradition. As a family moves away from having the legacy business as its center, it often has a setting that physically houses the extended family. While it can be a resort, the tradition of a shared family "place" with artifacts and spaces holding special memories for young people helps develop an identity beyond their particular nuclear family. It is often a place passed down by the founders, a grand old family home dripping with tradition.

Next generation programs don't originate spontaneously. They originate when a family member emerges to become the initiator or driver. This person can emerge from any generation:

- A family elder, perhaps a grandparent, who champions an active program for the next generation.

- A parent who sees common challenges in other branches of the family.

- One or more young family members, who want to know each other better and look to the family to develop meetings that include their generation.

We call a person who initiates this sort of innovation in a family enterprise a "family champion."[13] This champion then engages the family leadership to allocate resources for such a program.

The 4th generation of a European family (with approval of the 3rd generation elders), led by the head of their family foundation, began to hold such meetings for several days every two years. Like other such families, they had about 40 people—ranging in age from 40 down to 10, residing in a half dozen countries. They share a heritage, a family office with a non-family CEO, extensive investments, and a very public and extensive philanthropy program. Their goal was to "establish their own identity and debate their own issues." Some of them don't know each other well. By the second year, they formed several committees—family governance, philanthropy, and education—to develop themselves as the next generation of leaders in the family. A common vision emerged to anchor their commitment to sustain family unity for another generation.

Sustaining family community is not a single event; it is a process that begins slowly and develops over time, especially after a family death or transition. Here is one account of a two-generation development trajectory:

> We started on the process to develop a family constituency. We had five different branches who were close but their interests were different. When the third generation came along, we had to find out if we want to continue. My grandfather passed away in 1993 and all 19 G3 members got together for the first time. We did not grow up together. We decided there was something we wanted to do so several months later we got together to learn more about each other. It was kind of a touchy-feely type of thing. We decided that we were okay. I believe that participation by the next generation brought the family back together again. We started to ask if we were truly a family. If so, what do we need to do about the businesses to include those of the family? We brought in a consultant and started talking about the Family Council, and cooperation, coordination and listening to each other. We have been doing it 15 years but we have come a long way.

---

13 There is a longer Guest Commentary by researcher Joshua Nacht about family champions and how they create change in the family in Section Four.

WISE COUNSEL RESEARCH
44 WINDSOR ROAD
MILTON, MA 02186

DENNIS T. JAFFE, PH.D.
DENNIS@WISECOUNSELRESEARCH.COM
WWW. WISECOUNSELRESEARCH.COM

RELEASING THE POTENTIAL OF THE RISING GENERATION:

7

Choosing to be Partners

An extended family gathering enables the rising generation to decide whether they want to be partners, and if they do, what form their involvement will take. It is a fundamental building block of the 100-Year family:

Every two years our generation (G3) would all come together. 4th generation children would get to know each other and we debated the issues, looking at who is considered a family member, all the way to family values. There was a pretty good turnout, so it must have tapped into a real need.

We always try very nice places, in the mountains or the beach. Four or five of the thirteen members of the 3rd generation were driving it. We had a very high attendance. We talked about some of the issues about transition to third generation membership of the board, and thought about what we should do as a family office business and how we should look after an investment.

When you got together, were you already in control of the family affairs?

No. This is why we did this. It had not passed from one generation to the next. The second generation controlled the estate, which is still the major shareholder in the holding company. The initiative came from our generation agitating upward rather than the second generation saying we're ready to pass it on.

Our generation was more entrepreneurial, more direct in what we wanted. I advocated that we should have internal investment management skills around this big pool of assets. It took 15 years to complete that transition. We debated things like the structure of the holding company board, should there be a representative from each of the four family branches and should there be a family and a non-family deputy chairman. Gradually, all of these governance arrangements evolved. We thought carefully about who should replace whom, when. That 2G to 3G transition took a decade.

One family has what they call the "grandparents project", where grandparents teach and mentor their grandchildren. They retired from the business but now want to share their experience and spend time with their grandchildren learning from them about things like technology, as they share what they know as mentors:

The grandparents' camp came out of a meeting with an Indian family who had businesses. They were private businesses and they had businesses in different parts of the world. How do you get them to work together? We make sure that they have to share the same kitchen. We send the cousin generation away together. Because they're the ones that are going to be working together. And unless they get to know each other when they're young they're never going to be able to work together.

Several families mentioned how nicely grandparents fit into this role.

Extended family gatherings often include more than two generations. Today, with life expectancy rising, the family may have three or even four adult generations. The passing of leadership, responsibility and governance is not from one generation to another, but across two or more generations. It may involve different generations sharing leadership, in a complex power and responsibility arrangement.

WISE COUNSEL RESEARCH
44 WINDSOR ROAD
MILTON, MA 02186

DENNIS T. JAFFE, PH.D.
DENNIS@WISECOUNSELRESEARCH.COM
WWW. WISECOUNSELRESEARCH.COM

HOW LONG-LASTING FAMILY ENTERPRISES PREPARE THEIR SUCCESSORS

One major feature of these inter-generational activities is sharing and telling family stories. Older family members are invited to talk about their experiences, and family members use drawing, writing, video and social media to record these stories. By sharing the legacy young people develop as a community, and they are able to build upon the legacy as they re-envision the future.

8

A Roadmap for Family Development

This graphic is adopted from a family with over 100 family owners, including many who work in one of the various family businesses. It outlines a developmental sequence of activities that are offered to family members as they grow up and begin to exhibit interest and capability. The goal is to invite them to consider whether they might have the desire and capability to take a role in the family enterprises, and if they do, to plan their development accordingly.

All Family Members

Target		Purpose
All Family Members →	**DVD & Print** **Meetings** **Open House Tours** **Interaction**	Connection & Passion
16-30 year olds —	**Interviews** **Request for Information**	Personal Connection
Potential to excel —	**Internships** **Mentors** **Career Development**	Intentional Engagement

Potential Career Paths

WISE COUNSEL RESEARCH
44 WINDSOR ROAD
MILTON, MA 02186

DENNIS T. JAFFE, PH.D.
DENNIS@WISECOUNSELRESEARCH.COM
WWW. WISECOUNSELRESEARCH.COM

RELEASING THE POTENTIAL OF THE RISING GENERATION:

GUEST COMMENTARY

"THE CONNECTED BUSINESS FAMILY"

By Edward Thijssen

Most business families around the world face similar family challenges. As a family grows from one generation to another:

- The family will get bigger,

- The family will spread out over different cities and countries,

- Less family members will have an active role, and

- There will be more and more diversity in the family.

It becomes hence more and more challenging to keep the family community together.

Starting with the 2nd generation, each family should develop a cohesion plan that will highlight the value of being part of the family community. Thriving family communities are based on strong shared interests, shared values and shared beliefs. Once your family cohesion plan has been developed, it should clarify:

- The financial value of being part of the family community, and

- The non financial value of being part of the community.

A healthy family community will ensure participants receive more value than they contribute.

To have a community where family members are engaged, it's important to develop content, educational programs and initiatives that meet members expectations.

The most common initiative to drive family engagement are in-person events. But in today's globalized world, where families travel more and more and get geographically dispersed, it's increasingly difficult to organize regular in-person meetings. One family meeting a year is a great, but is it really enough to keep members engaged, informed and close to each other?

My family, being in it's 4th, 5th and 6th generations, was facing this challenge. So about 7 years ago, I asked myself the following question: "If communication and education are key for our long term family success, how can we deliver the communication and education initiatives, if meeting physically becomes more challenging over time"?

That was back in 2006. Facebook, Youtube, Wikipedia were coming up, so with a friend from another family (Edouard Janssen), we came up with the idea to build a secure online platform and app. A sort of Facebook, but just for our own family.

We built a platform were we could re-create an "online" version of our family, accessible at anytime and anywhere, be it from your browser or mobile phone. We designed different online groups for the different stakeholders:

- Family members,

- Shareholders/Beneficiaries,

- Family Council members,

- Board members,

- Family Office staff, and

- Family Foundation Board members.

Each stakeholder was assigned to one or multiple groups, depending on their role in the family. This logical structure enabled us to:

WISE COUNSEL RESEARCH
44 WINDSOR ROAD
MILTON, MA 02186

DENNIS T. JAFFE, PH.D.
DENNIS@WISECOUNSELRESEARCH.COM
WWW. WISECOUNSELRESEARCH.COM

HOW LONG-LASTING FAMILY ENTERPRISES PREPARE THEIR SUCCESSORS

- Share board packs, board meeting minutes only with board members

- Share confidential business news & updates, press releases, annual reports, quarterly financial statements, etc with shareholders

- Share product ads, video interviews of key executives and independent board members, competitor profiles, and other non confidential company related materials with all family members

- Share our family tree, family address book and family member profiles, with all family members

- Share regular family member news and updates, fun photos and videos with all family members

- Share educational materials and develop online courses for all next generation members

- Create a secure vault for each beneficiary with important personal information managed by the family office.

- Build a family archive

- Share family council minutes, agenda points and discussion items only with family council members

Very quickly, we realized other families had similar needs and that keeping a family together over time was a universal challenge. We decided to create a company, Trusted Family with a simple mission: help families to stay together over generations, and enable them to systematically identify and leverage their unique family legacy.

Edouard Thijssen is a 5th generation member of the Belgian family behind the Aliaxis Group, and Co-Founder of Trusted Family. Trusted Family provides technology and advisory solutions that drive family cohesion to over 90 Business Families and Family Offices around the world.

Pathways to Cross-Generation Engagement

Regular family meetings help family members get to know each other and consider what they can do for the family. The family meetings and the availability of family resources, like the family office, allow the meetings to generate specific action plans. For example, one 5th generation family offers young people three pathways for engagement.

- Plant tours and business events,

- Participate in the family council or a committee, and

- Apply to become shareholder observers of their independent board.

By the third generation, when trusts and other entities hold formal power and authority, the elder generation has limited authority to dictate to the next generation. They have to adopt a more collaborative attitude in getting their children engaged to consider how they want to be involved together:

WISE COUNSEL RESEARCH
44 WINDSOR ROAD
MILTON, MA 02186

DENNIS T. JAFFE, PH.D.
DENNIS@WISECOUNSELRESEARCH.COM
WWW. WISECOUNSELRESEARCH.COM

RELEASING THE POTENTIAL OF THE RISING GENERATION:

But it's the 5th generation trying to drag the 6th generation in and there isn't the same authority that comes from those older generation folks saying 'thou shalt gather.' When you have all these cousins spread out they're like, 'yeah I like you but I get on a plane and go home, I got kids in school and all that.' But when the grandfather was right there, when you have the senior guys and they were the big business leaders, this was very powerful. We don't have that anymore. And that was a lost opportunity from my father's generation .

9

Entry Rituals to the Legacy Family

Traditional societies hold rituals to mark major milestones, where an individual faces the community and is welcomed into a new role or status. The formal entry into family governance is one such transition that has great importance for the generative family and the individual. Several families developed formal rituals to make this passage:

We offer an invitation to younger family members when they turn 18 to be a part of these annual meetings. We've done some really good work around tradition and initiation and including younger family members, inviting them in a ceremony. It happens at the annual meeting for any new 4th generations. If you're born into the family, when you turn 18, you're invited to be a part of the business side. We hold a ceremony to introduce you, pairing the younger family member with a mentor from the older generation in a different family branch. We've have mixed success with that mentor program but I think the idea is really good and helping build relationships between generations and branches. That mentor introduces the incoming 4th generation family member to the family (enterprise), and that 4th generation member receives a ring that all of us have gotten at age 18. It's like a puzzle ring and it represents the six branches of the family all living together. That's a wonderful symbol.

My great uncle would always tell the story about the pioneers moving West and how they would throw their hats across the creek if they were traveling in their covered wagons. By throwing their hats across the creek, it's showing your dedication and commitment to cross that creek because a hat back in the old West was a big deal and you didn't want to lose your hat. You get a ring and you get a cowboy hat, and we find a little stream and make sure you have to cross. There was a lot of symbolism and connection and this initiation ceremony has been really valuable to younger ones. It's kind of the big deal to be invited in and to have all the family there to welcome you. The family office does an orientation to give you information on investments and business, before you show up. It's a lot of support around what is it that I'm getting into and this is welcoming of the family as well.

WISE COUNSEL RESEARCH
44 WINDSOR ROAD
MILTON, MA 02186

DENNIS T. JAFFE, PH.D.
DENNIS@WISECOUNSELRESEARCH.COM
WWW. WISECOUNSELRESEARCH.COM

HOW LONG-LASTING FAMILY ENTERPRISES PREPARE THEIR SUCCESSORS

Service Activities

Shared service activities offer an avenue for young people who have grown up with wealth, and may feel uneasy or conflicted about it, to focus on giving back to the community, helping build a further rationale for working together in a new generation:

> Going through this process creates family glue, which helps everything hang together in the future. Everybody has a hand in the creation, which means they bought into it more. This is another reason why it's got more likelihood to survive, as opposed to something created by one or two people. If others aren't involved in it, it doesn't have the same level of traction with broader family. Also, the broader family doesn't have any perspective to comment on or even identify the hidden issues throughout the whole plan. That was a function of our distance apart and (lack of) communication, which was difficult. Even though it sounds like we've done everything right, there's a lot of challenges to get it really right. The key is to have everyone involved.

Learning about the business can be active and experiential, especially for younger family members. One farm and food retailer has a unique way to promote their young 4th generation as "family ambassadors":

> We set up a store visit policy where we provide them with business cards as the fourth generation family member. We have a process where they visit a store as an ambassador for the family. We actually give them a little compensation for doing that. They can choose to do it if they want, as one way they can be involved. The company has stockholders. They have a travel fund, so they're encouraged to attend a food show or a family business conference. At the food shows from the time they were little, they could be in the booth meeting people, walking the show with grandpa or with dad or mom and seeing what the business is like.

Family learning might include educational travel. For example, one family conducted what they called the Asia Project, a cross-generational family group traveling for several months learning about social investment. Their learning has since had an impact on the expansion of the business and also the development of their philanthropic mission, less centered on their own home community. During these expeditions family members react to the deep emotional experiences of human need and social projects, and think together about what projects to adopt for their own family.

The rising generation become more than dutiful preservers of tradition. Generative families recognize that they have to focus on adaptation and change, rather than the status quo. Here is an account of a G3 family leader about teaching G4 the need to focus on the future:

> When working for the family, one of the things I've always tried to convey to them is you have to think of the office and process almost like an architect. You want to figure out what your end result should look like and work backwards to figure out how to build it. An architect is drawing a beautiful building, but you never start with 'Hey, let's look at our wiring and plumbing and cement'.

WISE COUNSEL RESEARCH
44 WINDSOR ROAD
MILTON, MA 02186

DENNIS T. JAFFE, PH.D.
DENNIS@WISECOUNSELRESEARCH.COM
WWW. WISECOUNSELRESEARCH.COM

RELEASING THE POTENTIAL OF THE RISING GENERATION:

After the 4th generation, we see more dispersed families having less connection even to their family branch, which means the new generation has less direct sense of each other, let alone as part of a unified group of partners pursuing a common vision. An important developmental activity in these families is getting together as a generational group. By doing this separately from their elders, they can comfortably develop their connection to each other. They often discover that due to their legacy, they have many shared values and things in common. They also find they like each other.

Getting together as a generational community offers an opportunity for the rising generation to make requests to the elder generation. As Millennials, they have a particular way of seeing the world. Learning about the family legacy and values, they have their own questions, concerns or requests. For example, several families report that after a meeting of the younger generation, they became comfortable sharing their concerns with their elders. By sharing them as a group, rather than individually, they do not risk one person being singled out as having a "problem"; they shared as a unified generational group, with the credibility that they should be heard because they will inherit leadership.

As family social and educational activities diverge from those of business oversight and governance, the family can decide to be more inclusive. Families discuss how, for example, to include married-in spouses. Here is how one family evolved toward more inclusiveness as they developed an explicit, formal governance process:

> For our cousin's camp, a decision was made that there would be no business meetings. We all grew up with our parents, the five branches. We would get together with our grandparents on Thanksgiving and Easter. After the meal, my grandfather would grab all of his kids and take them in another room and close the door leaving their spouses outside and the kids outside. There was never a participative type of thing for the rest of the family. The third generation said, 'We don't like that approach of separating spouses. Spouses need to be included.' We have made that change but we also want to make sure that everything that we do as a family is not strictly business. We want to make sure we still have social time. Since we have a two-day family assembly that is mostly meetings, we have another time that is strictly social, on the ranch. We want to share what the ranch does environmentally and taking care, stewardship and all the stuff we are doing. We don't want to have formal meetings at that time. We get everybody together, just for the fun of being around each other and enjoy it.

BUSINESS/FINANCIAL BRIEFINGS

Traditionally, family enterprise leaders and trustees are reluctant to share much information with family beneficiaries and the rising generation. The elders have a tradition of "taking care" of them and do not feel they need to be informed. This paternalistic model is common in many places around the world. But the family members we interviewed found this tradition did not properly allow for the development and engagement of the next generation. If they were not informed, how could they learn about the legacy and prepare themselves not just for possible employment in the business or other family activities, but for acting as owner/stewards in overseeing the assets, or contributing, often without compensation, to shared family activities? Our generative families **all** hold some variant of an annual business meeting, where family members of all ages are invited to attend and learn from the business and financial leaders.

WISE COUNSEL RESEARCH
44 WINDSOR ROAD
MILTON, MA 02186

DENNIS T. JAFFE, PH.D.
DENNIS@WISECOUNSELRESEARCH.COM
WWW. WISECOUNSELRESEARCH.COM

HOW LONG-LASTING FAMILY ENTERPRISES PREPARE THEIR SUCCESSORS

These annual events can be traditional one or two-hour presentations of business figures and charts, but many families found ways to make them far more elaborate and interactive. One family with a large business "produced a very detailed annual report, not unlike that of a public company, which we circulate to all family shareholders. The CEO and CFO present to all shareholders semi-annually. We have quite a detailed regional meeting. On the structured capital side, we distribute most of the profits as dividends, but if people want to reinvest, there's a Dividend Reinvestment Plan."

Meetings include visits to businesses, family office or foundation, and conversations with key employees. They are increasingly interactive and feature more than information, "Touring the company farms, plant tours, business center tours, and the museum; so that there's a good bit of hands-on activity to create interaction with what's actually going on in the company."

Family business education is not simply "delivered" by the elders to the younger generation. It combines leadership from the elders and active engagement from the younger generation:

Having a family that's committed to family education is essential. There needs to be a driver within the family pushing it. In the early days we held workshops on understanding personality types, communication skills, and financial things. Utilizing an outside source to provide some programming makes a huge difference because if you're trying to develop these things on a one-off basis, it's incredibly time consuming. Years ago we developed a longer-term curriculum of what we cared about having our kids learn. Then we looked at the components and identified the things we thought made sense for the kids to learn together in a common space or place. We then identified the things that we felt were better taught and learnt within the branches of the family.

Part of the education is learning about activities and roles which do not exist for a non-business family. The briefings clarify the differences between working in the business and being an owner. An **owner** has certain rights, with others delegated to members of the board of directors. An **employee** works in the business and receives a salary, but does not necessarily have a say in oversight or business policy. A family member can be an employee, an owner, or both. This can be very confusing, especially for young people initially exposed to the concept. Briefings define the roles of an owner, manager, board member, trustee, or family council member. For example, one family had a training program for prospective trustees for the family trusts. They had dozens of such trusts and each one needed successor trustees. The family wanted to appoint family members, but to do so, they needed to learn how to act as a trustee.

Another G4 family created an extensive business leadership class to orient new adults and married-in family members to the complex family enterprises:

It's a seven-week summer class held once a week where folks from our company come in and talk about their area of responsibility, what they do and the what they have in their history. They come to learn about the business. We hope that prepares them for college so they'll know what they want to do. Once you graduate from that class you can spend a week in the business shadowing people, doing a little deeper dive at what you heard, and a better understanding. We call this Production Group Experience and they work with people in the business and get exposure. Some employees work with them in the company. We say to them:

WISE COUNSEL RESEARCH
44 WINDSOR ROAD
MILTON, MA 02186

DENNIS T. JAFFE, PH.D.
DENNIS@WISECOUNSELRESEARCH.COM
WWW. WISECOUNSELRESEARCH.COM

RELEASING THE POTENTIAL OF THE RISING GENERATION:

'Tell them about who you are and your education. Tell them the challenges and only what you're doing in the department. Get them prepared for life a little bit.' That's another way we expose the kids before they get here.

Many families offer sessions where family owners, and some owners-to-be, ask questions and share ideas. Families also have longer sessions, where young family members (and sometimes people who have recently married-in) learn about the family and its various ventures. In larger enterprises, these seminars may last several days. The level of transparency is generally high, with families deciding that new generations will not feel connected unless they are informed. These families usually ask that those attending understand what is shared is confidential, not shared outside the family. The families in our study soundly endorsed the idea that, if they want the next generation to be involved, older leaders should share business information with the rest of the family. They view the next generation as their future owners and leaders, and educate them accordingly.

The interactive nature of the family meetings, where information is shared and family members air concerns or differences, also helps the family develop mechanisms to resolve conflict even in financial matters. As they get to know each other more deeply and share values and experiences, they develop a level of caring and trust that allows them to broach and even resolve differences that arise:

Ten years ago, our annual family meeting was fraught with conflict and stress which was a real burden. We began to implement a process for dealing with conflicted relationships or disgruntled family members; we call it our task force process. That is where we would get a question, which in the past would have caused an argument or a challenge. Instead of allowing that to be our pattern, we spent time answering that question. If it wasn't a ten-minute response we would actually get into a lot of the history and understanding the person's concern or complaint, and the policies or procedures that exist today that support whatever we were looking at. For example, one of the questions we got was 'why is the dividend policy the way that it is', which everybody knows is really the 'how come I don't get more money' question. Instead of shutting them down, we spent a year answering that question of why do we give dividends, how do we determine what that number is, can the company sustain its growth with this current policy, can the family sustain its growth with the current policy. It took us six years to get through all of the major questions and to demonstrate that we were willing to take people's concerns seriously and address them rather than allow those concerns to blow up into family conflict. We use that process today for implementing any kind of change. It's one of those really big moves that we made in our family. Through that task force process we built working relationships. From those working relationships friendships developed.

WISE COUNSEL RESEARCH
44 WINDSOR ROAD
MILTON, MA 02186

DENNIS T. JAFFE, PH.D.
DENNIS@WISECOUNSELRESEARCH.COM
WWW. WISECOUNSELRESEARCH.COM

HOW LONG-LASTING FAMILY ENTERPRISES PREPARE THEIR SUCCESSORS

EDUCATIONAL PROGRAMS

Regular family gatherings and business briefings are just the foundation for building the next generation. Members of the rising generation must learn and develop skills they will need to serve the family. Because of the size of the family and its special needs as a business family, the larger and longer-lived families in our research develop custom-built educational skill development programs. These programs go beyond information sharing to developing the *capability* to take on leadership in the many facets of the family enterprise. They teach the specific skills to become a productive steward of the family enterprise: leadership, relationship, financial and business skills. Unless they study business or finance, these are not skills one would gain in higher education.

Family education programs also focus on interpersonal skills like communication and can be similar to experiential corporate training, but with the trainees being family members. Like executives, they learn to work more effectively as a team, overcome (sibling) rivalry and not bring in conflict from the family:

> *Over the decade, we have done age appropriate work across a myriad of subjects, including self-development, leadership, understanding self, and basic entrepreneurial practices. We reviewed every acquisition we've conducted over that decade. We review our financials twice a year formally with them. They've gone through our tax return in detail and they have been to events that launch a new product, new rotation, grand opening, expansion of a site. When they were 14 years old we started talking about if they wanted to have a car they had to make $5000 on their own by say lifeguarding or cutting grass.*

> *We also designed a summer experience for teenagers where you spend time in all the finance, IT, HR strategic planning, human resources and small business initiatives. Some of them returned to their company and worked in areas that were particularly exciting to them. They entered college with an unusually deep appreciation for the complexities and opportunities it would take to be in the business world. I would call those very rich windows. You had a young person in an adult environment, listening and seeing the inner workings of a four-business-unit enterprise.*

A family member who works full-time as Family Relationship Manager, is tasked to develop the human capital of the now hundreds of family members:

> *Parents need to make sure they're talking about the vision and values around the dinner table. That's key. Once they get older and they become inquisitive, we have a whole set of things we do with the family. We start at age 12 and categorize them from age 12 to 20. We want some of the 20-year-olds to be the mentors to some of the 12-year-olds. We do functions with that age group two to three times a year. We call it 'cousin-palooza.' Education doesn't revolve around what we do, it revolves around who we are. You get these kids together and introduce them to each other and like: 'Hey, I know you; you sit next to me in science class. I didn't know we were related.'*

Education programs are frequently graded for age cohorts. Younger children and teenagers attend gamified activities, like a scavenger hunt or creating a family tree. One family used the word "generage" to refer to the members of a generation who were of similar ages. They designed programs for each generage.

WISE COUNSEL RESEARCH
44 WINDSOR ROAD
MILTON, MA 02186

DENNIS T. JAFFE, PH.D.
DENNIS@WISECOUNSELRESEARCH.COM
WWW. WISECOUNSELRESEARCH.COM

RELEASING THE POTENTIAL OF THE RISING GENERATION:

10

Basic Money and Wealth Management Skills[14]

Family education programs often teach young people core money management skills. These skills are important to all young people, but, because they are expected to become stewards of family wealth, the family teaches these skills to the family together.

How to...

1. Feel comfortable with wealth

2. Talk about wealth in personal relationships

3. Manage my personal wealth

4. Work with advisors

5. Save

6. Keep track of money

7. Get paid what you are worth

8. Spend wisely

9. Live on a budget

10. Invest

11. Handle credit

12. Use money to change the world

Another family created a financial skill seminar, initially offered to family members over 21. The first topic was about how to pay taxes. The second year the topic was budgeting. Younger family members expressed interest, so they lowered the eligible age to 18. Even more family members attended. Finally, for the third year on the topic of investing, they lowered the age to 15, and had their largest attendance. This family has a tradition of family engagement, but they have been struck by the interest of their younger members. They have begun to add to their pool of "future family leaders."

Family education may not only be about business. Other families have seminars on topics like natural resources or sustainability. When several members were moved by a new novel, one family invited the novelist to spend a day with them. These special learning activities are possible because of the commitment of the family to use its resources for shared learning.

These programs represent a significant investment of time, energy and money. Families report that they receive continual feedback about their value from young participants and their parents. Their goal is education not just to work in the business, but to take responsible leadership roles in governance, for example, as board, family council or family committee members:

Now that our family is bigger, more people are engaged in educating and developing skills that make them a viable board member. Our board's changed because our business has changed. The board oversees investments that are more complicated, and there is more to know and a lot more business experience needed than back in the old days when it was just a board with family members who just were there because they were family members.

The next generation program has its highest value because it is building a cohort of people who are getting educated about what we do, how the family council is structured and family history. They're getting educated about why we're awesome and why we need to continue to be who we are, embracing the values and

---

14 Adapted from Godfrey, Joline. (2008). **Raising Financially Fit Kids**, Random House, and from conversations with Jim Grubman.

WISE COUNSEL RESEARCH
44 WINDSOR ROAD
MILTON, MA 02186

DENNIS T. JAFFE, PH.D.
DENNIS@WISECOUNSELRESEARCH.COM
WWW. WISECOUNSELRESEARCH.COM

HOW LONG-LASTING FAMILY ENTERPRISES PREPARE THEIR SUCCESSORS

emotion around being connected to a family like ours. The next-gen program is inspiring the next generation of family members to pick up the flag and keep marching forward.

As households diverge, the family ponders how to promote attendance and participation in shared family events, with so many competing elements of their lives. As this 5th generation family leader observes:

Several things encourage people to come. Their children are now making relationships with their cousins and this program is built around the zero to 13 year olds and they beg their parents to go. Sometimes we hear back that the parents don't really want to go but the kids are very anxious to engage with their cousins. Not only are they getting their parents to come who might be on the edge, they're also creating this relationship with each other so that by the time they get into the boardroom or the family council or wherever they're going to plug in, they have relationships and know each other.

The families report growing attendance as the events become more regular. Over the years, more and more family members elect to come. Many families pay expenses and travel, and some even reimburse for missing work or baby sitters. The concept is that if this is an event that serves the family, people who are supporting themselves should be compensated for their time and expenses. If there are 100 family members, this can be costly, and the family has to decide what the benefit is for the family. Many decide that it is what they want to do.

The Family Academy

One US family entering its second century has developed family activities that exemplify the complexity of building a connected, capable and committed emerging generation:

We have a very extensive internship for high school and college kids. We have a mentoring program. At age 16, they attend the meetings and they're given a family mentor (other than their parents) to sit at the annual meetings with them, and meet with a couple of times throughout the year to answer any questions they may have. We started the annual Family Academy to educate kids four to 15-years-old. The family council works with the company to set up the agenda for the annual meetings; we get reports from our manufacturing and real estate divisions. Through the education committee and the coordinator of the family council, we have a cycle of topics for years to come.

We're a global company. We own land overseas and a shipping branch. We hear reports about what's going on and have activities that involve fun things with the company employees and the board who attend the annual meeting. Somebody in our family does videos to introduce the family to family members and things that they do. There's a lot of high interaction as we've gotten to know each other better; it's been really interesting to see the branch divisions dissolve. At first, we didn't even know who each other was, so one of the activities to get to know family was a placemat of the family tree. We would go around and try to figure out where everybody was. The young kids made a 120-foot long family tree and everybody stood on their square. We take our annual picture on it and every five years, they update it. Everybody could see where everyone was. When we first started big annual meetings, we had 110 people attending. When we started, people would come in and sit in their own little nuclear family group. Now, it's completely broken up.

WISE COUNSEL RESEARCH
44 WINDSOR ROAD
MILTON, MA 02186

DENNIS T. JAFFE, PH.D.
DENNIS@WISECOUNSELRESEARCH.COM
WWW. WISECOUNSELRESEARCH.COM

RELEASING THE POTENTIAL OF THE RISING GENERATION:

We were hearing from people, saying they didn't know how to read a financial report. The CFO and I put together a session on 'How to Read a Financial Report.' We have a cycle of topics and it came up to be a finance year. We asked, how do you teach business finance to a five-year-old? Every year the kids produce something. First year, it was refrigerator magnets. They've done bird houses, they've done book bags, just kind of use your imagination. The oldest members take on the role of CEO, CFO, COO because everybody has to be an officer. They take on these roles and do production teams cross age because we have from five to fourteen years old. At the big dinner, they sell what they produce and then the next day, they take their money and count it. Since the first year, we've opened a bank account for them. They always borrow from the company for their supplies and then they have to repay the supplies. They figure out their retained earnings and then take a percentage and donate it to charity. They make a financial report to the adults. They learn about all sorts of things. It's always great fun to see how the kids account for the foreign money. The first year, they just wanted to disregard it and I said, no, you can't just count that as a dollar. It's not a dollar. You've got to look up the foreign exchange, what's that? Let us show you. So they now know about foreign currency exchange.

MENTORING AND CAREER DEVELOPMENT

Mentoring is the pairing of a young family member with a more senior person who guides them to develop skills, a trusted person they can confidentially open up to about their misunderstandings and anxieties. The mentor can be another family member, an independent board member or non-family executive. Mentoring can be about development with the goal of working in the family business, but some families also offer mentors to those who are early in their careers and considering several options, as this young leader of her family council reports:

Our G4 are now reaching the age where they're ready for summer jobs and summer internships, as juniors or seniors in high school starting college. We created mentorship programs and summer job opportunities. We've made it a point to create opportunities for G4 to work in the business or to be exposed to the business at age 15. We've also been focusing on ways that we can educate our G4s about the business, what they're a part of and what they've been born into, along with talking them about wealth and stewardship and being good human beings. We're trying to improve ways to pass on our values.

Mentoring and career development serve a dual purpose: they help prepare for one's career of choice, and they also develop qualified family members for part-time governance roles. These programs offer an added benefit: being part of these efforts develop bonds of connection to each other and what the family is doing. They also offer visible opportunities for the rising generation to add to the family, social and business mission and demonstrate their leadership abilities to the rest of the family. Some elders report spotting family talent to recruit from the quality of their engagement and dedication to family education and meetings.

Mentoring can be formal or informal. It may begin informally within a single household:

Once a month we get together with my three children. Just to touch base and see whether the different activities of businesses are growing. Then twice a year, we have a full gathering, typically about one day — one day and a half in some place. We are quite spread around, and we get together, including all members of the family and the spouses and children.

WISE COUNSEL RESEARCH
44 WINDSOR ROAD
MILTON, MA 02186

DENNIS T. JAFFE, PH.D.
DENNIS@WISECOUNSELRESEARCH.COM
WWW. WISECOUNSELRESEARCH.COM

HOW LONG-LASTING FAMILY ENTERPRISES PREPARE THEIR SUCCESSORS

Mentoring is a special opportunity that a family can provide for even high school age family members, to prepare them for the challenge of career selection and preparation:

We try to meet and connect with each one of those kids in their twenties. We have a team called The Family Sustainability Team. Our goal is just to get to know them, find out what they're doing in high school, their goals are in life, what they want to do when they grow up, and where they want to go to school. And at the same time teaching what options might be there in the business. We try to connect with them before they start to get too far along in their college career or in the business world because we were having people apply for our business. I had guys and gals coming to me and one of them have a degree in landscaping and the other one's got a degree in music and history and I'm saying: 'They're not the skills we can use.' We were the employer of last resort, if they couldn't find anything else anywhere else. We want to stop that from happening. If they're interested in the business, let's make sure that they get the right education before they get here.

Young family members may feel the opposite of entitled. They may be concerned that they measure up, and need support from others to make effective career and life choices. This support can come from inside or outside the family. Here is one account of seeking support from a network of peers about developing confidence when starting work in the family enterprise:

I think it is more can I really do it? Of course, working here it is quite a big thing. It gives me a lot of sleepless nights. It is about getting at peace with the whole thing. Yes, it works, it is possible and I know it is a big thing. Even with this, even if you want to do it, it is quite a challenge.

It has to feel good that your Dad has the confidence in you. He wouldn't come to you with this if he didn't feel confident that you would succeed, right?

Yes, but still I have a lot of friends and I think it's helpful is to be part of a family business network because you always think you are the only person in the world who has such a crazy family and there are quite a few more who are even crazier. We say a lot of times that if someone would retire, or my Dad retires and he would look for a successor in the free market, you would not be chosen. Because of that gap you get the feeling 'I can do it because I have the skills and I am prepared.'

Career development does not come with am employment guarantee. Just being kin in a family enterprise is not sufficient qualification to work in a professional capacity. But with some training, a young family member may find a role in family governance or service. Their enterprises demand a high level of capability, even as a volunteer. Since the needed skills are somewhat unique to a family enterprise, they are not easily learned in formal education.

By knowing each other across families and spending time together, family members learn abut the skills and interests of older family members in other households and become comfortable informally seeking them out. So in addition to parents and siblings, a wider network of cousins, uncles, aunts and elders can be called upon. This is what is called "relationship capital". One family mentioned that there was hardly a college where a family member could not be found who knew someone who attended; this network might be of some help in learning about schools.

WISE COUNSEL RESEARCH
44 WINDSOR ROAD
MILTON, MA 02186

DENNIS T. JAFFE, PH.D.
DENNIS@WISECOUNSELRESEARCH.COM
WWW. WISECOUNSELRESEARCH.COM

RELEASING THE POTENTIAL OF THE RISING GENERATION:

Some families utilize non-family board members as mentors to family members in the business. Another family member, running the family office in a large 6th generation family, mentioned how young family members often came to talk with him informally. One family leader reported that he spends 60% of his time mentoring, meeting each week for an hour with each of a dozen family members working at various roles in the business.

Mentoring and career development take place both inside individual households and within the extended family. Some parents take the initiative to speak with their children about career and help them develop a career plan. This is important in legacy families as each young person needs to consider the important question of how they will participate in family enterprises, whether as employees or in governance. They are able to help their children look at the issues of entering or not entering the family business as compared to other opportunities, like working in the family foundation or serving on governance committees. Other families accomplish this by creating a whole family program. If the households in the family see this as a common challenge, they can justify using family resources; if not, they can do it within their household.

WISE COUNSEL RESEARCH
44 WINDSOR ROAD
MILTON, MA 02186

DENNIS T. JAFFE, PH.D.
DENNIS@WISECOUNSELRESEARCH.COM
WWW. WISECOUNSELRESEARCH.COM

HOW LONG-LASTING FAMILY ENTERPRISES PREPARE THEIR SUCCESSORS

GUEST COMMENTARY

"A FAMILY EDUCATION AGENDA"

By Meghan Juday

We developed a 10-year plan to grow our capabilities as family stewards to be the best possible partner to our fast growing company. To ensure success, we needed a deep bench of qualified family leaders and family director candidates. Everyone who is interested in becoming qualified for a more complex role has an Individual Development Plan (IDP) as a roadmap to role readiness for a responsible position in family governance.

To oversee and run this process, the Development and Education Committee (DEC) is responsible for:

- Helping individuals and the family grow their stewardship capabilities,

- Administer and coordinate all educational needs of the family,

- Coaching all family members who want to build competencies to be eligible for a new role,

- Managing individual development plans for those who are seeking a new role, and

- Providing meaningful feedback throughout the process and deliver a quarterly evaluation to each individual who is working towards a more complex role.

Below is an annual calendar of the educational activities coordinated by the DEC and delivered either by management or outside professionals. Our family business is extremely supportive, collaborative and transparent with the family and conducts multiple training sessions throughout the year:

Annually:

- One day of in-depth education conducted by CEO and CFO. Topics range from financial education to acquisition strategy,

- One-day management presentations with all of the Business Unit managers,

- Board round table with the family,

- Management round table with the family,

- One family council meeting is moved to another business unit; the meeting includes a factory tour and presentation from the business unit manager, and

- One family council meeting is held before or after a family business conference at the conference location.

Bi-annually:

- Financial case studies with CFO and Corporate Controller, and

- Outside educators conduct training during family council meetings.

Quarterly:

- Family receives the quarterly board packets – minus the detailed financials,

- Quarterly board debrief calls with the Chairman to review the board meeting and business performance, and

- Quarterly conference call with the CFO to review the quarterly financially.

WISE COUNSEL RESEARCH
44 WINDSOR ROAD
MILTON, MA 02186

DENNIS T. JAFFE, PH.D.
DENNIS@WISECOUNSELRESEARCH.COM
WWW. WISECOUNSELRESEARCH.COM

RELEASING THE POTENTIAL OF THE RISING GENERATION:

Meghan Juday is an enthusiastic champion for family business. Her dedication to the global family business community is rooted in her experience as the fourth generation leader and director of the IDEAL Industries family. It was there, that she developed a real heart for stewardship, evidenced in her work with families as principal of the Family Business Strategy Group and as director of the Initiative for Family Business and Entrepreneurship at Saint Joseph's University.

Career development can become the focus of family meetings, with the opportunity for the younger generation to learn from the older one:

> *One time, we gave the next generation the planning of an agenda, and they ended up creating a process where different people from G4 told stories about our careers. G5 was on one side of the room, G4 was on the other side of the room and there was an interesting dialogue back and forth about the things that are helpful at certain stages of careers. There has been an informal approach. It is hard particularly with people at that stage of their careers, to be involved in all of this family governance work. Almost all of G5 now have active careers.*

The generative family actively prepares the next generation for roles on the board, in family governance such as on the family council, or with the family foundation. In first and second generation families the board may include all or most family members. However, as the business and family grow and the board begins to include independent non-family professionals, family board members themselves require a higher level of professional skills, in financial oversight, strategic planning, and business development. The family has to develop such skills for future board members rather than just have the larger shareholders wait their turn to serve. Board membership is becoming a responsibility, not a right of family owners.

As more people participate in governance, the next generation has to learn make decisions together. Many families do not want to have a formal vote for policies, but are concerned to build consensus. This is difficult to achieve; working consensus requires a real commitment to compromise and listen to others. One 4th generation family leader notes how difficult this is for the emerging 5th generation:

> *Leaders are emerging but everyone's afraid to give anyone power, because we saw what happened with our parents, and we don't want that to happen to us. It might be with the best intentions, but if one person takes it the wrong way or it's misinterpreted, you might lose that person's trust forever. And you've lost credibility, because things don't really work in the family. Things have to be unanimous to work, which is very time-consuming. If you're not looking for consensus, you're going to fail; fifty-one percent isn't going to cut it. We had an opportunity a while back to install our water on the ranch. Not the water rights, but pump water and sell it for various drilling activities, which could have been a huge income source. But because it was viewed as something different, there's risk associated with it, and it's not going to happen. How do you overcome that? There's absolutely no easy answer. If there was, there wouldn't be books and books and books on this stuff.*

WISE COUNSEL RESEARCH
44 WINDSOR ROAD
MILTON, MA 02186

DENNIS T. JAFFE, PH.D.
DENNIS@WISECOUNSELRESEARCH.COM
WWW. WISECOUNSELRESEARCH.COM

HOW LONG-LASTING FAMILY ENTERPRISES PREPARE THEIR SUCCESSORS

12

Competency Development

Another family is more specific about how to prepare next generational leaders. By documenting the competencies needed for various family governance roles, they target their education programs to develop those skills. As an investment, the education program is accountable for results just as their business is:

We've outlined the expectations of each role in our family. We have expectations for our family assembly that give us a baseline for how we need to move that fifth generation up, in order for them to be good functioning family members. We've also articulated expectations for our family council role. We have 12 people in our family council who meet quarterly, and we see them as leaders of our business and the most active family members we have. In our governance model, we have standing committees, four people in charge of each standing committee. We've created expectations for all of these and we're working with a curriculum developer to build an education program.

There's a lot of different ways a person gets developed. We provide a curriculum. We have coaching and mentoring available. We have assessments that one can take advantage of to see their baseline capabilities. We have a development education committee that helps individuals put together development plans based on where they want to go. We have also an evaluation process to be able to measure whether or not an individual as successful in achieving those expectations and what additional support they need to meet those expectations. It's been very deliberate in developing our family and it's something the family agrees is vitally important for us to continue to be good stewards and to grow to be the stewards we need to be over time. This is now an on-going process because as the business achieves its goal, it's going to have another goal and that's going to be the moving target for us to keep moving ourselves.

Junior Boards

It is critical to prepare young family members to serve on various family boards, that oversee and develop their various enterprises. Board membership, while open to owners, is often delegated to the most capable people, including non-family independent directors. In order to serve on a board, a family member must learn the role and prepare for it. One way they can do that is by observing the board in action.

Several families created a program to give young family members an initial experience with governance, where they learn what is needed and decide if they see this in their future. This "Junior Board" takes several forms. Some families select young people who seem interested and capable, and offer them a role as an observer at board meetings. Other families open this group to volunteers, feeling that this is a way to discover a talent pool that has some interest in serving the family. This is not just for those who want to work in the business. Some family members will be needed to be part of governance—engaging in oversight by being on a board or family council. These roles attract some family members who are in graduate school, working at other jobs, or at home raising young children. The Junior Board may observe the board meeting, or have their own meeting that includes briefings and discussions with key members of the family business. One family had a quarterly seminar on "the business future" open to those who were willing to prepare by reading reports and reference material.

WISE COUNSEL RESEARCH
44 WINDSOR ROAD
MILTON, MA 02186

DENNIS T. JAFFE, PH.D.
DENNIS@WISECOUNSELRESEARCH.COM
WWW. WISECOUNSELRESEARCH.COM

RELEASING THE POTENTIAL OF THE RISING GENERATION:

Junior boards represent an entry point for becoming engaged in family leadership. Some legacy families have several businesses and entities with separate boards. One family with a large foundation and family office, invited family members to observe from the time when they were 14. The family leader observed, "We don't have a family farm or factory that people can visit. So this is what we do, and before they enter college, we want them to know what we do."

The family offers membership on one of these boards to younger members who express interest and capability. The effect of such engagement is to move from information sharing and education to put what is learned to visible use. By participating in these efforts a young family member can learn, but also demonstrate what they have learned. By taking on a project for example, overseeing a philanthropic investment, or helping a small company owned by the family, they develop a track record within the family. From these candidates, the family can select next generation members for various board and committee membership.

WISE COUNSEL RESEARCH
44 WINDSOR ROAD
MILTON, MA 02186

DENNIS T. JAFFE, PH.D.
DENNIS@WISECOUNSELRESEARCH.COM
WWW. WISECOUNSELRESEARCH.COM

HOW LONG-LASTING FAMILY ENTERPRISES PREPARE THEIR SUCCESSORS

GUEST COMMENTARY

"THE FAMILY BANK"[15]

By Warner Babcock

Wealthy families have substantial resources, that allow them to support family members beyond providing for the necessities. They can not only provide for a comfortable lifestyle, but also actively lead and support wonderful philanthropic initiatives, as well as explore some fascinating, unique life experiences and take on some uncommon risks.

While these wealthy families primarily think of their wealth and financial assets in terms of investment portfolios with overall investment objectives, goals, strategy, returns, allocation and acceptable level of risk, families are beginning to consider more seriously how to best use their financial resources to support the healthy character and development of future generations. This trend has begun to change the view of the overall perspective, planning and use of their resources. Discussion of their objectives, goals and portfolio allocation now includes allocating a portion of assets to the active development and support of future generations.

These include creating governance systems, mechanisms, policies and practices that allocate and guide a portion of their financial resources to specifically support initiatives for future generations.

One particular, effective approach wealthy families can take is to allocate a portion of their financial resources towards creating an internal "family bank" that makes family funds available under certain terms and conditions, and governance systems, to support future generations to buy a car or house, start a new business, or other useful, responsible purpose.

Senior family members usually form and fund the family bank. This can be done in the form of a corporate entity and/or trust(s) to address liability, tax, estate planning and/or governance issues.

There are five principles which can assist and guide families in discussing, developing and managing a family bank.

- They democratize, customize, flexibilize, harmonize, and professionalize the family bank.

- It is best to open up discussions with all parties early while developing a family bank so that all voices can be heard and all issues be considered.

- Each family and their circumstances are different, so each family bank should be uniquely developed and structured.

- Each generation is different, and circumstances change, so that the governance and terms should not be too rigid.

- All parties should work hard to develop and maintain healthy relationships at all times, as without this a family bank may have caused more harm than good.

- The family bank is like a family business, and evaluations, financial terms, policies, record keeping, reporting, and tax matters should be treated in a professional manner.

15 Babcock, Warner and Rosplock, Kirby. (2014). *Family Entrepreneurship and the Family Bank*, from Rosplock., K. (2013). **The Complete Family Office Handbook,** Bloomberg/Wiley, pages. 305-332; and Babcock, W. (2013). *Family Banks: Using Corporate Entities and Trusts, Trusts & Estates.* (April), and Babcock, W. (2012). *How to Properly Structure and Govern a Family Bank, Trusts & Estates.* (September/October), and Babcock, W. (2012). *Power of the Family Bank, Family Business Magazine.*

WISE COUNSEL RESEARCH
44 WINDSOR ROAD
MILTON, MA 02186

DENNIS T. JAFFE, PH.D.
DENNIS@WISECOUNSELRESEARCH.COM
WWW. WISECOUNSELRESEARCH.COM

RELEASING THE POTENTIAL OF THE RISING GENERATION:

When carefully designed, governed and managed well, a family bank can empower next-generation members to build human capital, develop their own wealth and learn to become good stewards of wealth, while continuing to build and maintain healthy family relationships.

The family bank can inspire and enable future generations to pursue their own passions, and become more entrepreneurial, A young family member may have an innovative idea, maybe a social venture, and the family bank and its governing body, processes and policies can offer an empowering and more disciplined approach, without having to involve external parties, who may not have the same values or patience.   With a good governance system in place, the family bank can become a powerful, sustainable entity that lasts generations to encourage responsible, effective development of future generations to make decisions together and support one another. Isn't that be a legacy worth having?

A family bank should be formed with good legal and tax advice, and with well thought out governance structures, a board, and clear objectives, goals, policies, criteria and agreements. All participating members should be able to clearly understand how the family bank works, and its processes and financing criteria and rules.

Here are a few additional factors to consider:

● A business plan with a financing proposal and other funding prerequisites should be required.

● Holding the borrowers accountable will serve the family bank and all participants well over the long-term.

● Intra-family loans should be made with the advice of tax experts.

● Independent oversight with a board of directors or review board can provide experience, fresh perspectives and objectivity.

Wealthy families now have the knowledge, foresight, resources and access to advisers to help them to redeploy their assets better today than ever before to support the healthy development and character of future generations in a more disciplined and responsible way using family banks.

Warner King Babcock is the Founder and CEO of the New York City Family Enterprise Center, Inc., and holds an Advanced Certificate in Family Wealth Advising and is a Family Firm Institute Fellow. He has advised family businesses and family offices for over 30 years and has been a member of a family council, family business CEO, board member, shareholder and trustee.

WISE COUNSEL RESEARCH
44 WINDSOR ROAD
MILTON, MA 02186

DENNIS T. JAFFE, PH.D.
DENNIS@WISECOUNSELRESEARCH.COM
WWW. WISECOUNSELRESEARCH.COM

HOW LONG-LASTING FAMILY ENTERPRISES PREPARE THEIR SUCCESSORS

Part Three described the breadth and depth of the shared family activities through which a generative family approaches the growth and development of their most important resource—the human capital of the rising generation--through four common family learning initiatives:

- Bringing the family together across generations to decide who they were and what they want to do together.

- Sharing information and teaching about the legacy and the family enterprises.

- Creating education programs for the rising generation to learn and grow together.

- Crafting skill and career development and mentoring programs for individuals.

Together, these activities are a unique feature of a generative family. In addition to informal family gatherings and relationships, a long-term family enterprise must work actively to engage, develop, and incorporate members of each successive generation into the various family enterprises. If not, the default is that they do not remain a legacy family much longer.

APPLYING WHAT YOU LEARNED: QUESTIONS FOR FAMILY REFLECTION

These questions can be posed to family members to begin a conversation related to the key ideas presented in Part Three.

For the Elder Generation:	For the Rising Generation:
• How do you help members of the rising generation feel part of the larger extended family descended from the G1 wealth creators?	• How have you become informed about the activities of the various family enterprises?
• Have you informed them about what the family offers and what it needs from them?	• What makes you want to participate? What holds you back?
• What are the opportunities available for the next generation to become engaged in the family?	• What is most exciting about being part of this unique family?
	• What is your plan for contributing to the family?

WISE COUNSEL RESEARCH
44 WINDSOR ROAD
MILTON, MA 02186

DENNIS T. JAFFE, PH.D.
DENNIS@WISECOUNSELRESEARCH.COM
WWW. WISECOUNSELRESEARCH.COM

RELEASING THE POTENTIAL OF THE RISING GENERATION:

PART IV: CALLS TO SERVICE OF THE RISING GENERATION

The goal of family education programs is to develop an empowered, inspired, capable, and ethical generation of stewards prepared and dedicate to continue the family enterprise. This takes more than maintaining the status quo and sustaining family wealth. The new generation is expected to **add** to the legacy, grow the many forms of family capital, and make their own mark in the world.

Every young person in any family has the opportunity to go forth and make their own way in life. "Find your passion," parents instruct their children. Prepare and develop skills to do something that will support and engage you. This is no less true for members of generative families. While the shared activities and business and service activities of the generative family have much to offer, successors can always go off on their own, and many do. Yet legacy families have an added potentiality. The rising generation also **has opportunities to serve the family.** This final section describes the "call" of these special opportunities within the family, that figure strongly in the life choices and developmental paths of young people growing up in generative families.

Generative families frame a family or community service invitation to attract those who are ready, willing and able to get involved. Keeping the family enterprises vital demands an increasing level of skill in each generation. Each generation prepares a new generation to do more than just maintain the legacy. They want successors who innovate as the business environment and family both change. The role of educational programs is not just to prepare the next generation, but to frame the message that calls them to take creative roles within the family and its multiple enterprises.

Every generation of elders can only create a **climate** consisting of inviting opportunities for the rising generation. In response, each member of the rising generation makes a **choice** to become part of it. Young Millennials today have been educated and raised in a cyber-world where they are globally connected. Growing up with wealth, they develop values about doing something significant. If they join the family enterprise, they usually don't do it just to honor the past and fulfill an obligation (though this may weigh heavily on them). *They often join to do something they cannot do elsewhere.* They want to set their own stamp on the family enterprise, even as they honor and respect legacy values and practices. They can always choose to go their own way, separate from the family. Joining is a commitment to give up some of their freedom in return for becoming part of a shared legacy and future success.

Family education and development efforts do not compel the new generation to serve the family. By creating an offer, a "call" for them to serve, they make it attractive for them to engage. This section presents the two unique "calls" a generative family offers the rising generation:

- The call to serve the family and family enterprise.

- The call to serve the community and the world.

The ultimate success for a generative family occurs when a critical mass of their rising generation answer each call to step up and become family leaders.

WISE COUNSEL RESEARCH
44 WINDSOR ROAD
MILTON, MA 02186

DENNIS T. JAFFE, PH.D.
DENNIS@WISECOUNSELRESEARCH.COM
WWW. WISECOUNSELRESEARCH.COM

HOW LONG-LASTING FAMILY ENTERPRISES PREPARE THEIR SUCCESSORS

The "offer" is that by virtue of their membership in the legacy family, members of the rising generation can do something extraordinary. The education and development process shows what has been done, how they can contribute, what might be done in the future, and the demands of the role. Each individual must make an active choice to respond to the call, and each does that in different ways. But the individual cannot make that choice if the family as a whole has not created the resources, structure and opportunities for them to be part of something great. This final section looks at how the rising generation can answer the call of the opportunity. Only if the new generation steps up, can the family succeed for yet another generation.

SERVICE TO THE FAMILY AND ENTERPRISE

Being born into a business family offers the opportunity to work in one of the legacy businesses, or with other family ventures, such as a family office or foundation. Career choices in any family are heavily influenced by the positive example of parents and relatives. If a parent is an actor, politician, craftsman, teacher, lawyer or farmer, one absorbs values and learns informally about these professions. Also, the benefits of having a network of people in that industry or profession enable an heir to enlist personal contacts for a possible job or career. Admission to the best schools, internships, and meeting the "right people" are all advantages to being part of a generative family.

In a family business, the opportunity is concrete and real. Family education and development has taught the rising generation about what is, and suggested what can be. The nature of the choice evolves as the family develops. Our research families that still owned the legacy operating business encouraged the next generation to work there, though they were not guaranteed that they would be promoted to leadership positions.

Each generative family was continually remaking itself, forming new business and social ventures and renewing or selling their legacy business. The rising generation has to become change leaders and be creative about the future.

Some generative families had non-family CEOs, and instead offered opportunity to

- Serve on the company or family office board of directors,

- Serve on governance committees and task forces,

- Start new ventures, or

- Serve as a volunteer, employee or board member of family social ventures.

This invitation is conditional on being professionally qualified and having the skills to be competitive in an often large, complex and specialized business. Almost every family had formal, or at least clear but informal, rules for employment. They dictate standards about qualification, background and preparation for entering the family enterprise. As the number of family members in each generation grows, competition for positions becomes greater and the demands higher.

WISE COUNSEL RESEARCH
44 WINDSOR ROAD
MILTON, MA 02186

DENNIS T. JAFFE, PH.D.
DENNIS@WISECOUNSELRESEARCH.COM
WWW. WISECOUNSELRESEARCH.COM

RELEASING THE POTENTIAL OF THE RISING GENERATION:

We heard four pathways by which the next generation became employed in the family enterprise:

- **They were asked to join by the business leaders.** The young prospect had visible success outside the business, and the family actively recruited that person.

- **They could ask to join.** They had to apply and be accepted by family and non-family leaders. They often joined at a low level with the expectation that they would be promoted as they demonstrated capability.

- **They "fell in,"** joining the business for convenience and then finding it comfortable and just remained there.

- **They were "pulled in."** It was expected and they simply joined. Very few families reported this pathway.

The top two pathways are by far the most common, as the business, by the third generation, has become large and complex and only those who can perform can find a place.

Entry is often not an all-or-nothing one-time choice; it is an evolving conversation in the family. Working in the business is an opportunity whose end point is not necessarily business leadership. But it does carry responsibility:

> I told my nephew everything I'm teaching you will make you extremely marketable whether you stay with us or go elsewhere. There is going to come a time at some point in the future, where I'm going to come to you and say, time to sign in blood. But until I do, you are free to come and go as you please, stay if you want to stay. Whether he stays in the business or not, he can be the person that carries on, that guy in the village. He doesn't have to work in the village to come back to the four meetings a year and know the village history. So, I haven't asked him for a commitment to be chief of the village yet.

Working in the business or family governance is not necessarily decided at an early career stage. Several families with well-developed family councils that oversee many households and complex family enterprises recruit leaders when they are older. Several parents who became family leaders mentioned they first raised their own children, then slowly become involved in family leadership. They now are at a time in life where they can be "of service" to the family, and the family values their expertise. This family leader was called to service after a career in non-profit management and after raising her family:

> It's a full time job. I work everyday, but the family members approached me and were encouraging me to consider (the job of family council chair). I worked as a legislative assistant for five years and so I had this interesting mix of political background and a non-profit background. My view of the family is you'd never want me to run the business, but I think the family is like a non-profit organization. It's really more of a non-profit entity. Once I started mulling over my own qualifications and having some cousins say, 'Well, you'd be good at this and you're well liked and you've had leadership roles and you're social,' I kind of went down the list, and had that conversation with my family. It was good timing for me in my life. I was just about to be an empty nester. So, that's how I ended up here.

WISE COUNSEL RESEARCH
44 WINDSOR ROAD
MILTON, MA 02186

DENNIS T. JAFFE, PH.D.
DENNIS@WISECOUNSELRESEARCH.COM
WWW. WISECOUNSELRESEARCH.COM

HOW LONG-LASTING FAMILY ENTERPRISES PREPARE THEIR SUCCESSORS

(Getting elected) was a pretty grueling process. It wasn't just a phone call saying, 'We think you're a great candidate, we'd like you to be family president.' I had to do interviews, I had to take tests, It was pretty incredible. I'm kind of surprised I'm here actually. It's daunting at times because you want to be able to communicate. It's so important to communicate with the family, but it's a lot of: people, personalities and different groups.

Preparing to be a family leader is different from being a business leader; it demands personal skills and capability, what we know of as emotional intelligence, EQ. Because of the personal relationships and history, working for the family enterprise entails having the ability to communicate and positively engage divergent views of family owners. Such skills are less critical when the business one enters is not owned by one's family. Family leaders must learn traditional business skills as well as "EQ" skills to deal with family relationships.

Successful families all reported that the bar for entry, the qualifications, increased every generation, as the business became larger and more complex, or the family moved from being an operator of a business to a financial or family office model. If they wished to enter the family business, the emerging generation learned they had to become a qualified professional. Just showing up would not do.

A few families reported a difficult transition, when the family removed unqualified or under-performing family managers. The shift from a model where the business was available to anyone in the family, to one where the family executive had to be qualified and accountable, was painful to some families, causing conflict between family branches. One family member reported a deep conflict over the firing of a family leader and his replacement with a non-family CEO. Because he was a valued family member and owner of a major share of the business, it took the active intervention of the next generation to help the family overcome the angry and hurt feelings.

The other shift is that while employment and business leadership was open to only a select few, many non-employment leadership roles are open to family owners: to serve on the board, in family governance or philanthropy. By the third generation, young family members looked to serve the family in all these governance roles, rather than primarily as employees. Some of these roles were voluntary and unpaid, while others had some compensation. Like employment roles, they required qualification and a level of skill.

One family decided not to have family members working in the business. The rising generation is expected to become involved in governance, common in families beyond the 3rd generation.

We don't allow the family to hold management positions in the company. So the majority of the seats are family seats in the board of the corporation, the family council, and the family foundation board which are today occupied by members of G4 and a small minority by G3. Management is professional with no family employees. We do offer family members internship opportunities and fixed-term job opportunities in the company. So we have an opportunity but also a challenge in the sense that it's not like we're always bumping into each other at the office and always together on business trips.

WISE COUNSEL RESEARCH
44 WINDSOR ROAD
MILTON, MA 02186

DENNIS T. JAFFE, PH.D.
DENNIS@WISECOUNSELRESEARCH.COM
WWW. WISECOUNSELRESEARCH.COM

RELEASING THE POTENTIAL OF THE RISING GENERATION:

Some families create a special role for family leaders working in the business. One 5th generation US business that owns several companies, with 24 family members working in the business, has an extensive support network and career development process for family employees. They can advance, but the corporate culture makes it clear that non-family executives do not step aside for less qualified family members. This family has an annual retreat for family employees and their spouses, which focus on bonding and also talking about the stress of combining family and business. There is a specific process for discipline, feedback, advancement and difficulties for family members, all of which are designed so that family issues and conflicts do not get transferred into the business. "The business is not designed to serve the family," the family "human capital" manager notes.

By the third generation, legacy families create a clear boundary and separation between the business and the family. Each has its own culture, policies and practices. While they are interconnected, membership in one does not necessarily bring membership in the other:

> We've done a very good job at driving home the family is family and business is business. One of my cousins asked to join the business, 'Yay, it's my cousin.' I'd like to help him, but when I sat down with my uncle and we discussed it, it really didn't make sense to either of us. He was completely unqualified and had no genuine interest or education. It's one thing if you have no education in what we do. We can teach you. But if you're not genuinely interested, we're not going to entertain that.

> We say you will work twice as hard as anybody else, take twice as much crap from the co-workers as anybody else, and get half of your worth on the open market. If you're still interested we'll talk. We really discourage family members so they can prove themselves.

Employment in the business is not something generative family members can count on. Rather, the call is for people who are prepared, have developed competency, accept and live the values of the family, and who are deeply committed to serve the family for the long term in its education, social and service activities, governance and family development roles.

WISE COUNSEL RESEARCH
44 WINDSOR ROAD
MILTON, MA 02186

DENNIS T. JAFFE, PH.D.
DENNIS@WISECOUNSELRESEARCH.COM
WWW. WISECOUNSELRESEARCH.COM

HOW LONG-LASTING FAMILY ENTERPRISES PREPARE THEIR SUCCESSORS

GUEST COMMENTARY

"THE FAMILY CHAMPION"
By Joshua Nacht, Ph.D.

True generative families create the climate for a range of opportunities for family members to be active and engaged stewards. One such role is what we call the "family champion": A rising generation leader who emerges from within the family-ownership group and works to develop the ownership, governance, and relational capabilities of the family-owners to support their goals of success. The family champion sees the opportunity and need to develop the family-owners to be responsible stewards, and takes on an increasingly engaged and influential role as a leader.

The family champion is a visionary catalyst who brings new energy into the system to support and develop the family-ownership advantage. People in this role are rarely designated or appointed by the older generation. Instead, they emerge of their own motivation and desire to make a difference in how the ownership group operates. In many cases, these people see that the potential negative outcomes that a lack of engagement from the family can cause, and begin to participate in a deeper way with their family. In doing so, they build credibility and trust amongst family members, thereby reinforcing their leadership role. This role emerges in a natural cycle as the family sees the benefit of family leadership, and rallies behind the family champion. The role commonly begins as non-positional authority without formal designation, but then evolves over time as the family sees the benefit of this leadership. Family champions often end up as family-council chairs or in a similar type of formalized role that makes their work even more effective.

The family-ownership group can be an important aspect of a successful enterprise by providing support, capital of all types, and stability to the business. Many members of multigenerational generative families find themselves in a position in which they own part of the enterprise, but do not work within it. The family-owners are faced individually and collectively with the challenge and opportunity of ownership of a legacy business. The pitfall is entitlement, and taking more out of the business than it can sustain. The potential success is a harmonious system in which the family and business contribute energy to one another, resulting in a long-lasting system. The owning family can be the source of valuable contributions of capital from people who have a true stake in the success of the family legacy. The family champion can provide the leadership necessary to help inspire, guide, and develop the family to be a true advantage to the enterprise.

Leadership within the family-ownership group takes place within a particular context. These families tend to be transitional as the family grows and evolves, multigenerational, have varying levels of ownership and wealth, have attendant family-dynamics issues, and are governance oriented in their influence and approach. Family champions display a range of skills and attributes that position them well for leadership within the family-owners. They have pertinent personal and professional experience that they can leverage for success. No one trains specifically to lead in this context, but leadership in other situations can transfer well. Family champions have strong interpersonal skills, most notably the ability to listen well, and to communicate effectively with a range of people. They have a strong sense of purpose about why they do the work, and help others create their own dedication. Family champions take initiative; they see the need for action, and answer that call. They build credibility and trust by being accountable, transparent, and authentic. These attributes

WISE COUNSEL RESEARCH
44 WINDSOR ROAD
MILTON, MA 02186

DENNIS T. JAFFE, PH.D.
DENNIS@WISECOUNSELRESEARCH.COM
WWW. WISECOUNSELRESEARCH.COM

RELEASING THE POTENTIAL OF THE RISING GENERATION:

are developed over time, and the most effective family champions engage in ongoing educational opportunities to grow their capabilities. Every family requires a different mix and flavor of these attributes, and each family champion is uniquely suited to the culture of their family.

The family champion plays an essential role in helping the family overcome the pitfalls of entitlement, and to instead become a tribe dedicated to a common goal. The family champion helps build a community of family members who are dedicated to being responsible stewards and building a family legacy by being actively engaged owners. This requires a lot of developmental work on the part of the family, who must attend to their shortcomings and family-dynamic issues that may be holding them back. The family champion helps the family develop their ability to communicate together, and to manage their intergenerational dynamics as strengths. While the family champion provides leadership, they cannot do their work alone, and empowering others to step up in responsibility is an important part of engaging the broad group. To effectively perpetuate their legacy, the family must develop a collective vision of what they want as a group, and leadership can provide a framework for this on-going conversation.

While not every family may have or need a "family champion" those who do have one or more people in this role tend to see some significant benefits. As individual leadership emerges and engages,

they inspire the family to be better owners. As the family–ownership group develops they are able to contribute to the success of the business through aligned governance structures, most commonly a family council and a Board of Directors. The result is an advanced family enterprise system, in which all of the parts are working in an increased capacity and function. The advanced system is more aligned, committed, and capable of being responsible stewards of the family enterprise legacy. This work is never 'done', and the cycle of engagement between individual, family, and business is ongoing and dynamic as circumstances change. Family champions attend to the continuous cycle, and help lead the family to become ever stronger as an ownership group.

The most effective, long-lasting generative families have a wide range of people playing complimentary roles. Leadership within the ownership group can be an essential resource to help the family meet their challenges and opportunities. Family Champions are catalysts who lead, inspire, and develop their multigenerational, complex families to be responsible, actively engaged stewards of their family legacy.

Joshua Nacht plays multiple roles as a steward, scholar, and consultant to family enterprises. His 2015 dissertation focused on the role of the family champion and rising generation leadership in business-owning families.

WISE COUNSEL RESEARCH
44 WINDSOR ROAD
MILTON, MA 02186

DENNIS T. JAFFE, PH.D.
DENNIS@WISECOUNSELRESEARCH.COM
WWW. WISECOUNSELRESEARCH.COM

HOW LONG-LASTING FAMILY ENTERPRISES PREPARE THEIR SUCCESSORS

SERVICE TO THE COMMUNITY

Young people are tied to the family not simply by expectation of financial rewards, which are a given. Rather, they decide to serve the family because of the opportunity to add their personal social values and aspirations to the collective actions of a great family. By the third generation, a generative family has come to focus its energy beyond creating wealth. They have done that quite well. Now answering the question, "What is our wealth for" takes on a new urgency. The answer that emerges from the family is that we have created huge resources that now offer emerging generations opportunities to participate in family philanthropy, and initiate new efforts that have both business and social value (e.g. social entrepreneurship). From the three boxes of the piggy bank of childhood, now a family member can participate in adult giving that makes a difference in the community and the world.

Many young people today are dedicated to social innovation, sustainability and service to the community. Of course, these values are often shared by previous generations, but the way these values are acted on differs in each generation. One generation gives to service programs in their local community, the next generation wants to help global refugees. The rising generation becomes part of the family enterprise with the expectation that the family will listen to their ideas and commit to actions for social goals. They want to see the family wealth used responsibly to make a difference, and they have very specific ideas for how they do that. When they enter, they often make these preferences known. To sustain their commitment the family has to have a process for making decisions and taking action. When it comes to social and community service, the next generation expect to have an active voice.

Young people are attracted to shared family philanthropy for several reasons:

- The family has resources and a network for making a difference, and they can have more impact together than separately,

- Their family is respected and visible and they can do service that is valued by their community, showing that they are not just "trust fund kids,"

- Because of the family's wealth, they are able to take on a role in a non-profit or job that does wonderful things, but does not pay well, and

- The rising generation has personal bonds with others in their generation and they like working together. They build generational community by doing something valuable, special and concrete.

The focus on "social capital" engages and inspires the living generation, as the family focus shifts from business operation to a more passive asset management:

> I saw in (the rising generation) that there wasn't anything to really rally around. Initially we started to engage family members at the family meeting in a discussion about philanthropy and shared plans. We asked, 'What do you do and why does that excite you and what organizations do you find?' That morphed into people wanting to do collective philanthropy. At that meeting we came up with parameters of how to do coordinated giving through our philanthropy division, and appointed a chief philanthropy officer, a CPO, who's going to be a part-time employee with accountability and specific guidelines in place.

WISE COUNSEL RESEARCH
44 WINDSOR ROAD
MILTON, MA 02186

DENNIS T. JAFFE, PH.D.
DENNIS@WISECOUNSELRESEARCH.COM
WWW. WISECOUNSELRESEARCH.COM

RELEASING THE POTENTIAL OF THE RISING GENERATION:

13

Uniting the 6th Generation through Community Service

Here is an account by a family whose business, recently sold, was situated for more than 100 years in a small town. Without the legacy business, the family was able to renew their connection for another generation by developing an extensive philanthropic commitment:

There was tremendous symbiosis between a growing company and the small town. Its values, informed the values of the company and helping the small town. Family members grew up with a very strong sense of responsibility, and commitment to the community.

We started talking about philanthropy as one way to keep a family together. Out of one of those meetings came the genesis of the Community Fund. A few of us got together and raised $10,000 when we passed the hat amongst our generation. It focused initially on kids at risk and we've made the mission a little broader as we grew. We wrote letters to the broader family and then we received contributions from G5 that added assets. Now we're giving to 30 organizations in the area. We have ten board members from all branches of the family. At the beginning it was a lot of blood, sweat and tears where each of us would read the grants. The family office was incredibly helpful in administering the fund. The only requirements to be on the board was to give a little money and to be willing to contact organizations that applied for grants to learn more about them, write that up, make a case why we should support that particular organization, follow that organization, and stay in touch with the organization.

This led to people who didn't have a lot of connection coming back to the larger family. They got quite excited that they could have relationships with these organizations. Over time, we've been able to hire a part time executive director. Now we're giving grants directly to service organizations. We're giving capacity building grants, convening meetings. We're about to go off to a big family gathering in June. This process has kept our family together for at least another generation.

WISE COUNSEL RESEARCH
44 WINDSOR ROAD
MILTON, MA 02186

DENNIS T. JAFFE, PH.D.
DENNIS@WISECOUNSELRESEARCH.COM
WWW. WISECOUNSELRESEARCH.COM

HOW LONG-LASTING FAMILY ENTERPRISES PREPARE THEIR SUCCESSORS

APPLYING WHAT YOU LEARNED: QUESTIONS FOR FAMILY REFLECTION

These questions can be posed to family members to begin a conversation related to the key ideas presented in Part Four.

For the Elder Generation:	For the Rising Generation:
• What do you do to keep open the possibility of family engagement for all members of the rising generation?	• What are the benefits to you of being part of this family?
• How are members of the rising generation informed and invited to participate in family activities?	• What attracts you about becoming engaged in family activities?
• How have you created a fair and open process for selection and accountability for roles in the family enterprise?	• What do you offer the family that might contribute to its success in the emerging generation?
• How do you offer your guidance, help and support to the next generation without them feeling the pressure to please you and do what you want?	• What would you most want to see the whole family accomplish in the coming years?

WISE COUNSEL RESEARCH
44 WINDSOR ROAD
MILTON, MA 02186

DENNIS T. JAFFE, PH.D.
DENNIS@WISECOUNSELRESEARCH.COM
WWW. WISECOUNSELRESEARCH.COM

RELEASING THE POTENTIAL OF THE RISING GENERATION:

CONCLUDING THOUGHTS

We've taken a long and deep journey through the multi-generational experience of 70 global families who have sustained and grown their various family enterprises for more than three generations. Their stories are inspiring and useful.

Your final task is to look at your own family enterprise (or if you are an advisor, the families you advise) and consider what you can do to lead your family down this path. Here are ten action steps that can be taken by any family that desires to thrive over generations as a generative, legacy family.

1. Your family has been successful in business and generated family wealth. Now you need to *decide as a family how you wish to use this wealth,* for its highest and best purpose. You can choose to invest some of the wealth in the tasks described herein, creating a generative family. This choice means that you will commit time, energy and resources to this task, and involve the whole family.

2. *Become engaged and ensure that this is not a task you outsource to others.* It is as simple as creating a family values statement or a financial literacy program for your children. These are important but only as part of a larger shared family project. This has to be done by you, working together to make it happen.

3. *Begin preparing the rising generation for the family's wealth through efforts in each individual household with their young children.* As a family, you can make it possible to talk about what it means to be privileged, and how to use the special advantages that wealth brings to the family. You can do things together that reinforce the family values such as service or a modest lifestyle, by your example.

4. A major step forward is to *convene a cross-generational family meeting or meetings* to talk about the future path of the next generation. The first meeting should be well-planned and last long enough for everyone to get to know each other, learn the history of the family and the family businesses, and talk about a vision for the future.[16]

5. Develop a *clear and explicit extended family values, vision and mission statement.* This expresses what you want to achieve together as an extended family, and sets out how you will do this. The values should be clear enough to guide behavior, and the vision and mission should be clear and concrete enough to guide decisions. The family may have values, vision and mission for itself, as an extended family, as well as its businesses and other enterprises, such as the family foundation. But as each generation reaches adulthood, the values have to be reinterpreted and the vision and mission refined and updated.

6. *Inform and educate the rising generation, in stages as appropriate, about the history, nature and structure of the various family enterprises.* The rising generation should learn about the family trusts, businesses and philanthropic ventures, and most important, about their obligations and responsibilities to the family, if they choose to participate actively.

---

16 Jaffe, D. and Allred, S. (2014). **Talking It Through**. Merrill Lynch.

WISE COUNSEL RESEARCH
44 WINDSOR ROAD
MILTON, MA 02186

DENNIS T. JAFFE, PH.D.
DENNIS@WISECOUNSELRESEARCH.COM
WWW. WISECOUNSELRESEARCH.COM

HOW LONG-LASTING FAMILY ENTERPRISES PREPARE THEIR SUCCESSORS

7. *Support each individual to actively develop a life plan for personal and career development.* For a young person emerging from a wealthy family, this can be a difficult task. The family should recognize that this is not easy for some, and offer support and resources when they are growing to adulthood to launch themselves, and also to decide whether they want to become actively involved with the family in various roles.

8. *Convene the rising generation to get together and decide what they want for the future, and in what way they want to be involved in the family enterprise.* They should get to know each other and make an active choice to be family partners and work together.

9. *Develop an active task force and organization to develop programs for the education and development of the next generation, with adequate family funding.* This task force or committee is usually integrated with a family council and other family governance activities.

10. *Set clear goals and criteria for the next generation and assess annually whether they are being met.* Knowing what people think helps to anticipate and talk about differences, rather than keeping them underground. It also helps you assess how you are moving toward shared goals.

This paper hopes to inspire and guide your family to make the choice to become a generative family, and then to begin the difficult, but gratifying, process of embarking on that journey across generations.

WISE COUNSEL RESEARCH
44 WINDSOR ROAD
MILTON, MA 02186

DENNIS T. JAFFE, PH.D.
DENNIS@WISECOUNSELRESEARCH.COM
WWW. WISECOUNSELRESEARCH.COM

RELEASING THE POTENTIAL OF THE RISING GENERATION:

Acknowledgements

Many people have given of themselves for this project. The research team of interviewers include Peter Begalla, Emily Bouchard, Jane Flanagan, Charlotte Lamp, Isabelle Lescent-Giles, Susan Massenzio, Joshua Nacht, Michael O'Neal, Jamie Trager-Muney, and Keith Whitaker. They also offered comments at various stages of development of the manuscript.

Others who have commented include James Grubman, Jay Hughes, Greg McCann and Christian Stewart.

I would especially like to thank Stacy Allred, David Begley, Valerie Galinskaya, Greg McGaulers and their colleagues at Merrill Lynch, who stepped up and supported this project, and offered many hours of feedback and help at each stage, including: Peter Hillsman, Phoebe Massey and Kristy Tridhavee.

Thanks also to Warner Babcock, Meghan Juday, Madeline Levine, Joshua Nacht and Edouard Thijssen for writing vignettes to amplify the quality of the narrative.

WISE COUNSEL RESEARCH
44 WINDSOR ROAD
MILTON, MA 02186

DENNIS T. JAFFE, PH.D.
DENNIS@WISECOUNSELRESEARCH.COM
WWW. WISECOUNSELRESEARCH.COM

HOW LONG-LASTING FAMILY ENTERPRISES PREPARE THEIR SUCCESSORS

About the Author: Dennis T. Jaffe, Ph.D.

For 40 years, Dennis has helped families overcome personal and organizational challenges to enable successful and fulfilling transfer of businesses, wealth, values, commitments and legacies across generations. As both an organizational consultant and clinical psychologist, he is one of the architects of the field of family enterprise consulting. He works with multi-generational families to develop governance practices and capability of next generation leadership, and to develop the capability of financial organizations and family offices to serve their family clients. He is an active speaker and workshop leader in programs for business families and financial service firms.

As a member of Wise Counsel Research, he is conducting this study of long-term family enterprises, resulting in working papers, *Good Fortune: Building a Hundred Year Family Enterprise, and Best Practices of Successful, Global, Multi-Generational Family Enterprises.* This paper represents the third phase of that project. He is part of the Polaris team, which is working with the Family Business Network to create a roadmap for family and business sustainability. With his global focus, he has taught at Hult University in Dubai, helped the Pacific Asia chapter of Family Business Network develop a program to empower next generation family members, and is on the Advisory Board of Chinese University of Hong Kong, and Stetson University.

He helps financial advisors and wealth managers develop skills to serve the personal needs of their client families. **The Values Edge,** an acclaimed tool using values cards to create a personal values pyramid, helps many families and organizations explore personal and organizational values. **The Family Enterprise Assessment Tool,** which helps business families compare their perspectives on ten key competencies for business and family success, has just been released as an on-line tool for families and their advisors.

He received his BA in Philosophy, MA in Management and Ph.D. in Sociology from Yale University. For 35 years, Dennis was professor of Organizational Systems and Psychology at Saybrook University in San Francisco, where he is now professor emeritus.

As a member of the Family Firm Institute since it was founded, he has presented at annual conferences, served on their board, designed and delivered continuing education courses in *Family Governance* and *Family Wealth Advising,* written frequently for their journal *Family Business Review,* and received the *Richard Beckhard Award* for his contribution to practice. In 2007 he was named *Thinker in Residence* for S. Australia, helping the region design a strategic plan for the future of entrepreneurial and family businesses. In 2010 he was a visiting professor at the undergraduate family business program of Stetson University.

Dennis has written a trio of books that guide members of family enterprises, including the 2010 book *Stewardship of Your Family Enterprise: Developing Responsible Leadership Across Generations,* as well as *Working with the Ones You Love: Building a Successful Family Business; Working with Family Businesses: A Guide for Professional Advisors.*

He contributed to the Campden Research Study *The New Wealth Paradigm: How affluent women are taking control of their futures,* and 2004 JP Morgan study of best practices of multi-generational families. His research on the governance of start-up companies, *After the Term Sheet* is an important contribution to the field of entrepreneurship. He has been a frequent contributor to periodicals such as *Family Business,*

WISE COUNSEL RESEARCH
44 WINDSOR ROAD
MILTON, MA 02186

DENNIS T. JAFFE, PH.D.
DENNIS@WISECOUNSELRESEARCH.COM
WWW. WISECOUNSELRESEARCH.COM

RELEASING THE POTENTIAL OF THE RISING GENERATION:

Private Wealth, Journal of wealth Management, and *Worth.* In 2005 he received the Editor's Choice Award from the *Journal of Financial Planning* for his article on family business strategic planning. His work was featured in *Inc.* magazine, *Entrepreneur, Nation's Business, Time* and *The Wall Street Journal,* and he was profiled in *People* magazine.

During the 1980s Dennis was an architect of the field of organizational transformation and development of change leadership. He wrote a dozen influential management books, including *Getting Your Organization to Change, Rekindling Commitment,* and *Take This Job and Love it!* As founder of *Changeworks Global,* he guided organizations and family businesses to lead long-term change by unleashing the power of their employees. He is the co-creator of *The Transition Curve, StressMap,* and other tools that support personal and organizational success.

For three years, Dennis was co-editor of *The Inner Edge,* a magazine focused on spirituality in business. He was deputy director for research at the Macarthur Foundation sponsored Healthy Companies Network from 1992-95. As co-founder of the web firm *MemeStreams,* he pioneered on-line executive development tools. The video *Managing People through Change* was voted one of the Best Products of 1991 by *Human Resource Executive. From Burnout to Balance* (retitled and reissued as *Self-Renewal*), and *Healing From Within,* were each honored with the Medical Self-Care Book Award.

Active as well in non-profit governance, he has served on the boards of the World Business Academy, Saybrook University, and the Center for Mind-Body Medicine, and as President of the Association of Humanistic Psychology. He lives with his wife Cynthia Scott in San Francisco, and has three sons and three grandchildren.

WISE COUNSEL RESEARCH
44 WINDSOR ROAD
MILTON, MA 02186

DENNIS T. JAFFE, PH.D.
DENNIS@WISECOUNSELRESEARCH.COM
WWW. WISECOUNSELRESEARCH.COM

HOW LONG-LASTING FAMILY ENTERPRISES PREPARE THEIR SUCCESSORS

About Wise Counsel Research and the 100 Year Family Enterprise Research Project

Wise Counsel Research is a public charity and think-tank devoted to researching and sharing the role of wisdom in contemporary life. We study family flourishing amid wealth, giving within families, the impact of wealth on women, and the role of advisors to enterprising families. We also regularly write, speak, and offer workshops on these and related topics.

Some of these workshops include programs focused on developing the potential of the rising generation, communicating between generations about estate planning, and managing family trusts. Members of Wise Counsel also offer courses on these topics at Vanderbilt's Owen Graduate School of Management as well as at other institutions. Wise Counsel offers a series of seminars on the topic of 'Living Well' that incorporates presentation, discussion, and ongoing consultation for people who have enjoyed fulfilling and established careers and are contemplating the question 'what's next' in life. Members of Wise Counsel also customize educational sessions for individual families on the topics of our books, including *The Cycle of the Gift*, *The Voice of the Rising Generation*, and *Family Trusts*, in addition to the results of the 100 Year Family Research Project. For more information about any of these opportunities, please contact Dr. Keith Whitaker at keith@wisecounselresearch.com or (617) 272-6407.

In its fourth year, the 100 Year Family Enterprise Research Project has made impressive strides. The publication of the second working paper *Good Fortune: Building A Hundred Year Family Enterprise*, led to widespread dissemination of our analysis of the first wave of interviews of successful 100-year families. We have had opportunities to present the findings at forums all over the world, and have had our research reported in a variety of publications, including *Private Wealth*, *Family Wealth Advisor*, and the *New York Times*. The report is available on Amazon in print and Kindle versions.

The Project has also collected an archive of family interviews and resource materials, including family constitutions, mission and values statements, and other materials that our respondents have shared with us. This archive represents one of the most significant collections in the world of materials on successful families. It will continue to grow and provide a resource for ongoing research projects for years to come.

WISE COUNSEL RESEARCH
44 WINDSOR ROAD
MILTON, MA 02186

DENNIS T. JAFFE, PH.D.
DENNIS@WISECOUNSELRESEARCH.COM
WWW. WISECOUNSELRESEARCH.COM

RELEASING THE POTENTIAL OF THE RISING GENERATION:

About Merrill Lynch, the sponsor

Merrill Lynch Family Office Services provides ultra-high-net worth families with highly sophisticated solutions designed to manage the complexities of substantial wealth. Family Office Principals work closely with each family, their Merrill Lynch Advisor, accountants, attorneys and other advisors to seamlessly implement a comprehensive approach that encompasses the family's overall financial, lifestyle and legacy goals and values. Merrill Lynch Family Office Services becomes a family's essential coordinator, counselor and support staff, delivering a streamlined experience allowing them to pursue personal aspirations knowing that experienced, dedicated professionals are focused on their affairs.

The Center for Family Wealth Dynamics & Governance™ at Merrill Lynch works collaboratively with wealthy individuals, their families and their advisors to be intentional about the impact of their wealth on themselves, their family and their community. The Center's mission is to empower ultra-high-net-worth families to nurture the different dimensions of wealth and to be purposeful about sustaining their wealth and values across generations. The Center provides thought leadership around financial education, family governance and family legacy, heritage and philanthropy, and facilitates family meetings to address top family goals and relevant issues.

WISE COUNSEL RESEARCH
44 WINDSOR ROAD
MILTON, MA 02186

DENNIS T. JAFFE, PH.D.
DENNIS@WISECOUNSELRESEARCH.COM
WWW. WISECOUNSELRESEARCH.COM

HOW LONG-LASTING FAMILY ENTERPRISES PREPARE THEIR SUCCESSORS

For print copies of this report, please contact:

Wise Counsel Research
44 Windsor Road
Milton, MA 02186

www.wisecounselresearch.com

To contact Dennis Jaffe for inquiries, questions and speaking and workshop events:

dennis@wisecounselresearch.com

Made in the USA
Coppell, TX
22 January 2022

72059903R00048